MIND OVER PLATTER

A new and different psychological
approach to the problem of
how to stick to your
reducing diet and
then maintain your
proper weight.

by

Peter G. Lindner, M.D.

foreword by

William S. Kroger, M.D.

Photograph by Horn/Griner; courtesy of Abbott Laboratories

Published by
Melvin Powers
WILSHIRE BOOK COMPANY
12015 Sherman Road
No. Hollywood, California 91605
Telephone: (213) 875-1711

Printed by

HAL LEIGHTON PRINTING COMPANY
P.O. Box 3952
North Hollywood, California 91605
Telephone: (213) 983-1105

Library of Congress Catalog Card Number 63-19738
Printed in the United States of America

ISBN 0-87980-099-2

CONTENTS

CONTENTS

FOREWORD

Nature and technology have combined to provide Americans with the highest living standard in the world. Food is so plentiful that programs have had to be devised to curtail crops and store surplus grains to prevent glutting the market and depressing our agricultural economy. Despite these drastic measures, however, our grocery markets are crowded with such a profusion of basic and exotic foods that visitors to our land gape with wonder at an abundance unknown anywhere else on earth.

We would have to be exceedingly ungrateful, as many foreign visitors have pointed out, to rail against this state of affairs inasmuch as starvation exists in other parts of the world, but the fact remains that this abundance is a mixed blessing. In some respects, the American dream has come true with a vengeance.

When President Kennedy recently stated that many Americans have become soft through lack of exercise, the implication was that this softness had been augmented by the systematic ingestion of fattening foods. The availability of rich foods is an irresistible temptation to approximately 50 per cent of our adult citizens who fight intermittently against weight problems. About half of these individuals are seriously overweight and are prime candidates for the degenerative diseases that lead to early death.

Unlike the major killer diseases which have foundations supported by the public, obesity is considered exclusively the problem of the individual and he is allowed to dig his grave with his knife and fork, undeterred by information and methods which would help him understand the compulsive nature of his destructive habit. He is as helpless when confronted with a platter of food as an alcoholic when confronted with a drink.

The compulsive eater, like the alcoholic, is aware of the consequences of his habit, and he tries to avoid the penalties involved by dieting. It is impossible to go to a social function these days without hearing interminable discussion about diets—one-day diets, one-week diets, one-month diets or even six-month diets. These diets may vary greatly in listing the foods an individual may or may not eat, but they all have two things in common. Their success depends on will power and the expressed or implied promise that the individual may resume his "normal" eating habits as soon as he has lost the desired number of pounds.

The result of all this is that a great number of Americans are always threatening to start dieting, complaining because of the restrictions of a diet they are already on or rejoicing that they will soon be able to "fall off" a diet that has made their lives miserable from the beginning. It will always be this way as long as the use of will power is the only way one can be successful.

Dr. Lindner, in the following pages, presents a program that realistically avoids the use of will power in attaining an ideal weight and maintaining it. Having treated 2,000 patients for weight problems, he is aware that the imagination is a far more potent factor in treating obesity than will power. His program is made even easier to follow by the use of self-hypnosis which by-passes the critical nature of the conscious mind and utilizes the automaticity of the subconscious mind to make dieting a pleasant as well as rewarding experience.

No matter how many times you have failed in previous attempts to diet, you owe it to yourself to try Dr. Lindner's methods. I can tell you from more than 30 years of personal experience that they work, especially when combined with a psychosomatic approach, that is, the best possible combination of drugs, if needed, and psychotherapy of a nature that the general physician is best able to administer because he best knows the needs of his patients.

William S. Kroger, M.D.

Beverly Hills, California

Chapter 1

Why Most Diets Fail

You Are Free to Indulge

OH, NO, NOT ANOTHER BOOK ON OBESITY!

The above exclamation may have been your first reaction when you saw the title of this book since it is undeniably true that a great many books have been written on overweight and obesity, and more are coming from the publishers all the time.

Newspapers and periodicals have added to this profusion of literature on the subject, and it sometimes seems that everybody in the United States must be trying various types of "crash" diets lasting anywhere from one day to six weeks. But none of the present expositions on this subject seem anxious to tell the fat or near fat individual that he will probably have to maintain some sort of restriction on his diet for the rest of his life. This is because few obese individuals want to hear such a prophecy since they feel they could not carry such a program to completion. This is the precise reason another book is needed in this already crowded field.

MOST DIETS USELESS

Regrettably, all the diets now available in print are bought with anticipation, read with interest, tried with hope and discarded with disillusionment. They all demand sacrifices the average overweight or obese individual is not prepared to make since he feels he can only make these sacrifices for a limited time. A new approach to one of our most alarming national problems is needed.

Statistics show there are now approximately 128 million adults in the United States and some 50 per cent of them are overweight. More than half of the latter group are obese, which means they are dangerously overweight, and the end is not in sight. Despite the fact the sale of reducing aids of all description add up to a billion-dollar-a-year business, our per capita weight keeps rising. There is a reason for this and you will learn it in these pages.

TYPES OF DIETS

In almost every one of the numerous books on obesity, emphasis is placed on various types of diets and different ways to manipulate calories. Many of them point out various ways of manipulating the three types of foods; namely, proteins, carbohydrates, and fats. Basically, however, every one of these systems of dieting always ends up with one major premise: The obese person must change his present method of eating. In other words, he must change his habits. He must go on a special type of diet. Many of the proponents of various diets begin by saying, "Eat all you want and lose," or, "Don't count your calories." These are catchy slogans because they represent the unconscious wish of every fat person, but when the diets are analyzed, one finds that there are always certain restrictions which make the projected goals difficult to achieve. The obese individual may eat all he wants of certain foods, but he is asked to avoid other foods and stick to a restrictive dietary program.

I cannot deny that I am in complete agreement with the fact that a fat person must follow some type of dietary program in order to lose weight, and it is not the purpose of this book to argue the pros and cons of the various regimens prescribed by others. Suffice it to say, any dietary program must be individualized for each patient. Your physician is the one best qualified to do this. A printed diet sheet can never replace personal professional guidance.

Why, you ask, have all these programs failed? In every instance, the individual prescribing the diet tells you what you *must* or must *not* eat, yet very rarely does he tell you *how* you can do it, and stick to it.

The main purpose of this book, then, is to show you how you can learn to *stick* to your diet, the one that your doctor has recommended in your specific case.

LOOK TO LONG TERM RESULTS

If you have a weight problem, you may argue that you have stuck to a dietary program a certain length of time and lost so many pounds. But the chances are, sooner or later, you regained your weight. Statistics show it is a rare individual indeed who is able to maintain his weight at the lowest level achieved by diets of any kind. Recently an article appeared in one of my medical journals in which the author followed up a large group of patients who had been on various types of reducing programs. At the end of two years, only two per cent had been able to maintain their weight at the new reduced level when left to their own devices, without medical supervision.

The methods of maintaining your correct weight which I will describe in this book may be contrary to many of your fallacious beliefs. It may be contrary to what you have read elsewhere. The views expressed here may be directly opposed to many long held theories. They were popular but never proved. The methods set forth in this book have all stood the test of time. They have been personally used by me and my patients. I do not think that anyone who has not had an overweight problem is qualified to write about obesity. One cannot possibly know the problems involved unless he has experienced them himself.

The things that I am going to tell you will be based particularly on personal experience, and the experiences of many of my patients. I thank the latter for the many things they have taught me regarding the problems of obesity. It was only because I faced this problem with my patients from day to day, year after year, that I was able to evolve the proven methods outlined in this book.

THE ACTUAL APPROACH

The contents of this book have been divided into three major sections as follows:

The first section will deal with some theory, and a presentation of the problem as I see it. It will be based on personal experience and not upon the writings of others. Just enough theory will be explained to give the reader an understanding of the methodology involved in combating this problem.

The second part of this book will be devoted to the actual modus operandi of the procedures necessary to enable you to stick to your diet.

The last part of the book will briefly outline some of the ancillary methods and actual dietary programs. I want to make it clear, however, that the suggestions made in the third part of this book are simply general guides and rules. Only your personal physician can outline a dietary regimen which is both nutritionally sound and designed in such a way that you will lose weight. This is a highly individualized matter and must be decided by a competent professional man.

My purpose is to show you how you can follow the diet that has been prescribed for you. Not only will I teach you how to stick to your diet for a few months, but I will tell you how you can adhere to it with minimum effort the rest of your life. But you must realize by now that you have a life-long problem, and it must be approached from this view-point. I am mainly interested in showing you that it is pos-sible not only to lose weight, but to keep that weight from coming back once you have lost it.

I hope that by the time you finish the book, this point will be clear to you. You will then be able to start on the actual techniques I describe. You will be amazed how such simple and easy-to-learn procedures can get results. If these tech-niques add to your mental and physical health, as I am sure they will, I will be well repaid for the many hours taken from a busy medical practice in order to write this book.

FAT IS SOCIALLY UNACCEPTABLE

It may be well to add here that being overweight has no com-pensations although you have heard and may even have tried to convince yourself that all the world loves a fat man. This phrase was coined by slender people who feel guilty because they actually believe that obese individuals are really unat-tractive gluttons who could be "cured" if they quit stuffing themselves every waking moment. If you don't think this is true, don't question your slim friends too closely. They may tell you the truth.

Our American culture is actually more kindly in its thoughts about alcoholics, for these people, some five million of them, are considered to be ill, and numerous apologists such as Alcoholics Anonymous, psychiatrists and psychologists have made their heavy drinking more socially acceptable than food excesses.

EVERYBODY CAN'T BE SLENDER

To be perfectly truthful, it is not possible for everybody to achieve the willowy ideal which has now been incorporated into the American dream of personal perfection. Even minor variations have become socially unacceptable, yet there is a paradox here because most people do vary from the cultural standard now prevalent. The painfully thin female clothes models are good examples, for instance, of what the average American woman would like to emulate.

This places a heavy burden on the physician who, unlike the reducing salons and pill purveyors, must determine those for whom weight reduction is indicated and those for whom it is contraindicated. He must, additionally, decide how *much* weight should be lost by those who want to become slender.

Part of his answers, of course, are decided by hereditary factors. The general nature of your body structure and nervous system are inherited, and a raw-boned individual with a massive body structure can never diet enough to look really slim. Every individual, however, can attain the body weight that is best for him, but this correct weight must be determined by a physician, preferably one that has been serving his family for a number of years.

SET REALISTIC GOALS

I stress these hereditary factors so that you can avoid the discouragement which is certain to set in if you seek to attain an impossible goal. Most people *can* become slim but those with large frames must content themselves with the correct weight for *them*.

There are many reasons for dieting aside from the improvement it makes in your appearance. Mortality figures show that obese persons have shorter life spans than persons of "normal" weight because of an apparent predisposition to diabetes, hypertension, atherosclerosis and heart disease.

I mention these things so you will approach a diet sensibly and adopt reasonable goals set by your physician. The purpose of this book is not to by-pass your personal physician, but to show you how you can stick to the *individual* diet he prescribes for you.

It should be mentioned here that our American society works against those who would remain slim by producing every type of food cheaply and abundantly. Luxury foods, which are essentially fattening, augment our basic foods in equal abundance, and it takes strong motivation to avoid the continual snacking so common with most of us. The Chinese, subsisting mostly on unpolished brown rice, may look close to starvation in our eyes but they show scarcely any evidence of the degenerative diseases that afflict middle-aged Americans. The availability of "sweets and treats" makes it more difficult for us to abstain.

None of the above has been written to discourage any one from adopting a dietary regimen suitable to his needs. Indeed, if you are carrying excess weight, you *must* reduce or pay severe penalties in physiological and psychological disorders. The fact that it may not be wise for you to attempt to slim down to the proportions of a fashion model, male or female, should not deter you from seeking to attain the best weight for *you*.

In closing this chapter, I am happy to add that most people *can* become slim and stylishly trim if they learn the methods by which this ideal can be achieved. That is the real purpose of this practical and concise book.

Chapter 2

Paradoxes in Dieting

One Man's Meat is Another Man's Poison

YOU'RE FAT BECAUSE YOU EAT TOO MUCH

I am sure you have heard this phrase many times. You may agree with it or make violent objections, but the fact is the statement is absolutely true. Let's analyze it, putting the accent on the important words, and see if you don't agree.

YOU are fat because YOU eat too much. The emphasis is already on YOU. Since YOU are reading this book, I assume YOU are overweight. Aside from physicians, few people who are slim read books on obesity. But let's continue. YOU are overweight because YOU eat more than YOUR body requires, at least at the present time. Strangely enough this does not mean that the same amount of food you eat would make someone else gain. In YOUR specific case YOU are putting more fuel into YOUR body than it can utilize, and the excess is stored as fat. Someone else, with different nutritional needs, might very well lose weight on the same amount of food. The thing to remember is that each person has a different weight problem and it must be treated on an individual basis.

Now that you recognize that the same amount of food may make one person gain and another lose, let's look at a few examples of how this works out.

THE MAN WHO COULDN'T GAIN WEIGHT

Not long ago I was asked to give a lecture to a large group in Los Angeles. The lecture was preceded by dinner. Sitting next to me was another physician who was to introduce me to the audience. My talk was to be on obesity and I recall thinking that what I had to say would be of little interest to my fellow physician who was tall, lanky and obviously not suffering from a weight problem. However, I always make it a practice to watch the eating habits of nearby diners, and in this case I watched my lanky friend and his wife, who was attractive but quite obese and food conscious.

Before the soup arrived my friend polished off three rolls, using his own and his wife's butter. She, of course, was watching her weight. When dinner was served, he ate quickly, cleaned his plate and then asked his wife if he could have her baked potato. She complied and the waiter brought more butter and another roll. After eating this extra ration, he looked around hungrily for more and wound up by eating his wife's side dish of corn and mine as well.

The main course was followed by lemon meringue pie and he topped off his gastronomical feat by gobbling up his own, his wife's and mine inasmuch as I, too, watch my diet. During the meal he drank three cups of coffee, each with three teaspoons of sugar and a generous amount of cream. At the conclusion, he appeared well satisfied but far from bursting as might be expected.

I was so fascinated by this performance that I asked him if he had starved all day in preparation for the heavy banquet meal. "Oh, no," he replied. "I had a big breakfast of orange juice, cereal with cream and sugar, two eggs with bacon, three slices of toast with butter, and coffee." He then added he had also had his mid-morning snack of a jelly doughnut and a glass of milk.

Further talk uncovered the fact that he had attended a business luncheon which included two highballs, pork, apple sauce, French fried potatoes, two slices of buttered toast and pie a la mode. He then returned to his office and later went out for coffee and chocolate chip cookies. As if this were not enough, he informed me he would eat again before going to bed, probably "a large sandwich, a malted milk and a candy bar with nuts in it." Well…

I remember my sympathies were with his wife who had not eaten all day in preparation for the banquet. She informed me it was discouraging to watch him eat the foods she enjoyed but could not partake of herself. Incidentally, he kept up this eating pace every day.

I have gone into this episode at some length to illustrate that one man's meat may be another man's poison and vice versa. There is just no predicting how much food an individual may ingest without gaining weight nor do we have adequate explanations as yet as to how these variations take place. It is extremely unlikely that such a person would ever gain much weight. Maddening but true for those who must limit their food intake.

THE UNKNOWN FACTOR

Just the opposite of the man above is the one who seems to gain weight on even the most minute portions of food although I must add that these people have a tendency to minimize the amounts they eat. By and large, however, they do eat less and gain more. Their food expenditure is exactly the opposite of those who come to me asking for a diet that will allow them to "put on some weight." I have been able to get some of these individuals to gain but I always find, on encountering them a year or so later, that they have lost it again.

From what you have read so far, you can see that losing or gaining weight is a complicated affair, and the phenomenon has not been satisfactorily explained by our medical investigations thus far. I have frequently put both types of patients through numerous tests involving metabolism and glandular function, and invariably their tests are normal.

THE "DOLLY SISTERS"

Here is another case involving twin sisters who were referred to me for obesity and whom my nursing staff always lovingly referred to as the "Dolly Sisters." These two very pleasant patients were identical twins and were the same height and weight. They lived together and were both working in the same department of an aircraft plant. Therefore, they were in each other's presence almost 24 hours a day. Here was an excellent opportunity to observe the results of a diet in two persons exactly alike, since they both had the same amount of activity.

Not only had they similar habits, energy expenditures, and sleeping patterns, but each could observe the other's actual food intake. If there were going to be any deviation from the diet, one sister would immediately point it out to the other. I asked each of them to keep a notebook of what they ate. Each week I compared their food diaries.

They were both placed on an identical 1,000 calorie diet. To my utter amazement, at the end of three months one sister had managed to lose 13 pounds while the other had gained 8 pounds. These two patients were put through the usual series of glandular and metabolic tests and were both found to be normal. This again points out the fact that two persons, regardless of how similar they are, may have different caloric requirements. Here, we have another paradox that modern medicine has, as yet, not explained.

An interesting study has been done by a pediatrician who studied a large series of children in a boarding school. She arbitrarily divided these children into three groups. The endomorphs (the short, stocky, broad type), the mesomorphs (children of average, normal body structure), and the ectomorphs (the tall, slender, lanky type). Since these children were in a boarding school, their dietary intake was closely controlled and could be closely observed. At the end of one year, the pediatrician recorded the most amazing results. She found that the endomorphs ate the least and the ectomorphs ate the most. As you can see, even in childhood, there is a variable food energy requirement for different youngsters. This is something else that must be explained by medical science.

THE NURSE WITH THE SWEET TOOTH

One more interesting paradox is exemplified by the following case of an attractive nurse, Mary Anne, who ate a great deal of chocolate candy at Christmas time. There is nothing unusual about eating sweets at that time of year except that this particular girl always stirred up much comment and envy among the other nurses. The candy would be located at the nurses' desk and all could freely partake, but Mary Anne did more than her share in depleting the supply. The envy was aroused by the fact that she never gained an ounce through her overindulgence.

The paradox in this case was provided by her past history. Three years earlier she had been referred to me for obesity, since she was 50 pounds overweight. She was placed on a reducing diet. For many years prior to her first consultation, she had experienced much difficulty in attempting to lose weight and had always gained her weight back. She lost the 50 pounds on a reduced caloric intake, and was then placed on a weight maintenance program. However, the most peculiar thing happened about three months after she started the maintenance diet. Because it happened to be Christmas, the patient started to deviate from her diet, eating many sweets and other high caloric foods. When she came in to be weighed in January, to her and my surprise, she had not gained any weight. It was then that she commenced to realize that regardless of the amount or kind of foods she ate, it was almost impossible for her to gain weight.

It has been three years since that time, and the patient now belongs to the group of people who are unable to gain no matter what they eat. Naturally, she is quite happy, but I am still astonished and have no answer to the riddle.

THE MYSTERY OF THE SURGEON'S WIFE

The other case is that of a 26-year-old wife of a well-known Los Angeles gynecological surgeon. Prior to her marriage, about five years before I knew her, she had had an obesity problem and had to be extremely careful about what she ate. Since her marriage, however, she had not encountered any further difficulty; in fact, she had gotten so thin that she tried to gain weight. Her husband is rather obese, but on many occassions when I personally observed both of them eat, she always ate more than he did. She usually consumes more than anyone else at her table. On questioning her husband, he remarked that she consistently devoured foods in large amounts whether she was eating out or eating at home. I mention this because it is often claimed that such people eat very little at home. The wife, of course, has been most delighted with her new-found freedom, but no physician has ever been able to find an explanation for the sudden change.

If we could explain just exactly what happened to the metabolism of the body in these two instances, it would probably throw much light on the obesity question. Notwithstanding, at the present time, if you happen to "get fat easily," you must resign yourself to the fact that the only way that you can lose is by cutting down your energy intake.

Thus, you should be able to realize that individualization of your diet is extremely important. That is why, throughout this book, I recommend that you place yourself under the guidance of your personal physician. He will plan your specific dietary program which will have to be adjusted to your precise needs. After that I expect that you will follow the system outlined here so that you will be able to adhere to the regimen necessary for you to lose weight.

EXERCISE ALONE IS USELESS

You have already seen that one way to lose weight is to cut down your intake of energizing foods. Now, what about increasing your output of this energy? Suffice it to say, exercise is an absolutely useless method of losing weight unless it is accompanied by a dietary program. If you were to walk 36 miles, you would lose about one pound. Chances are that after having walked this distance, your appetite would have been stimulated to such an extent that you would quickly replace this, plus more. A 300-pound man who walks up 15 flights of steps needs to eat only one slice of bread to replace the energy that he has utilized in his physical effort.

I can hear you saying, "But you are all wrong. Last Sunday I played tennis for three hours and I lost four pounds." You must remember that you probably perspired freely while you were playing tennis. Most of this loss represents a loss of water. This will be immediately replaced upon proper fluid intake and will have no effect on the actual loss of body fat. Since it is the latter that you wish to dissipate, your four-pound loss is really of little value.

"IT'S MY GLANDS"

Almost every week, I see one fat lady, referred to me for obesity, who starts out by saying, "Doctor, I know it must be my glands because I eat like a bird." Of course, most of you have already heard the stock answer, "Yes, I know, like a vulture!" I am sure that you have read many times that glandular problems cause only three to five percent of obesity problems. Therefore, increasing your energy output by administration of glandular extract alone is usually of no value. There are certain instances, however, where this is used as an adjunct to reducing. It will be explained in the last portion of this book.

PHYSIOTHERAPY IS NOT THE ANSWER

For similar reasons, you can readily see that sweat cabinets, exercise machines, or massage treatments are of no avail. I am always amazed to see how many patients will subject themselves to the discomforts of various reducing machines. They hope that someone else can do something to cause them to lose weight. Unless these measures are accompanied by a diet, they are absolutely fruitless. Until these patients realize that they must do something, they are sweeping the problem under the rug.

I remember very well the 56-year-old obese lady who consulted me, complaining that she had spent $800 on various types of reducing machines, all of which were now stored in her closet. As is often the case, she remarked during the initial interview: "I hope that you can take this weight off of me. I have tried everything." I knew at once she had to change her attitude. I was not going to do anything to her, but she was going to learn to do it herself. After she mastered the techniques outlined in this book, she lost weight very well. She is now one of the staunchest supporters of this program. However, she is still left with two problems: First, she needs to buy a fresh wardrobe for her slim, trim figure; secondly, she must find enough closet space among the discarded reducing equipment to hang all of her new garments.

The point I have been trying to make in this chapter is that *your* weight reduction involves different methods and diets than those used by other individuals. That is why the general diets prescribed for all in most of the books on obesity cannot be used in specific cases. Indeed, some of the diets I have seen, particularly the short term crash diets, are potentially dangerous. Do not ever follow a diet that has not been selected to meet your individual needs. After you obtain such a diet don't worry about how you are going to follow it. That *is* something you can get out of a book—this one.

Chapter 3

Will Power Won't Help

Mice, Men and Dieting

THE BASIC PROBLEM

Although reducing the energy intake is the basic problem in obesity, you must concern yourself with the sources of failure. These may be divided into constitutional and psychological causes.

Perhaps it never occurred to you, but your taste buds are one of the main reasons you overeat. In my many years of treating overweight patients, I have yet to find one who will overeat a food that does not taste good. The foods that the patient does not like are never a problem. The ones that taste good are the source of all the trouble. There has been some scientific work done which indicates that it is possible an overdeveloped gratification for the taste of certain foods may have an hereditary basis.

Recently, a group of scientists found that certain strains of mice had what they termed, the "obesity trait." They found that if they mated mice with this trait, a certain number of their off-spring would always be obese. They, thereupon, took two of the mice which were obese (presumably having the trait in their genes) and slimmed them down with a reducing diet. These mice were then mated. A certain percentage were again obese. They also noted that the obese mice in this group ate too much. When the scientists cut down their food intake, they all lost weight until they were normal.

The investigators then decided to carry the experiment a step further. They added quinine (a very bitter chemical) to the food of the "normal mice." They found that these mice initially ate only about 10 percent of the amount of food that they had previously eaten. Yet, within two or three days, they gradually returned to their normal food intake. The scientists then concluded that the normal mice ate because "they needed to survive," and not because "they liked the taste of food."

When the quinine was added to the food of the obese mice, they also initially ate only 10 percent of their food. However, at the end of one or two weeks, the obese mice were still eating less than 50 percent of their original food intake. The investigators then concluded that the obese mice ate, not because "they needed to survive," but because "they liked the taste of food." This trait of liking good tasting food was apparently hereditarily transmitted and actually responsible for the previously so-called "obesity trait."

It is true that further work needs to be done in this field, especially with humans. Nevertheless, it is an interesting discovery and in accordance with our clinical impressions during the course of medical practice. You will note later in the book that the subject of the taste of foods will become quite important in our therapy. At this point, I simply want you to be aware that, regardless of other contributing causes of your overweight problem, the food must taste good or you will not eat it.

"IT'S ALL IN YOUR HEAD"

Very rarely can you read an article or a book nowadays without being confronted by the statement that obesity is caused by psychological factors. I wish to disagree to some extent. True, there are a certain number of people who overeat because of deep-rooted psychological entanglements. However, I believe that they are in the minority. Most obese people do not have emotional problems as their main cause of overeating. This is like the old chicken and the egg dispute. Which came first? Obesity or the emotional issue?

The fact that has always amazed me most is that whenever I have helped an obese person reach his normal weight and maintain it for at least two years, most of his psychological problems cease to exist. Therefore, I am inclined to believe that the psychological problems of many overweight people are, more often than not, the *result* and not the *cause* of their overeating.

To illustrate another aspect of this dilemma, I am reminded of a couple that I have been treating for about 10 years. These two people were known to me prior to their marriage. I did their premarital counseling, then treated both husband and wife after they had been married and finally took care of their children. The husband had always been somewhat thin and the wife had always been a bit heavy. Nevertheless, each one of them kept their weight about the same in spite of continuous endeavor to normalize their respective weights on their own through the use of will power.

About five years after they were married, the husband suddenly lost his job due to a lay-off by one of the local aircraft factories. This created quite a financial hardship on the family. The husband became very tense and nervous while struggling to find another job. During this period of time, he lost most of his appetite and dropped 15 pounds. His appearance was now very thin. In time, his wife became upset because her husband was so apprehensive, but gained about 12 pounds during the same period. When the husband finally secured another job and the financial situation cleared up, he gained back the 15 pounds and his wife lost the weight she had put on. It is interesting to note that the same set of anxiety-producing circumstances may cause one person to gain weight and another person to lose. There is an individual factor involved that apparently decides which direction the weight goes. Therefore, it is erroneous to state that a certain type of emotional situation is necessarily followed by weight gain.

There *are* certain mental factors which may contribute to failure in a person attempting to adhere to a reducing diet. These are the ones I wish to describe briefly at this point. They are factors which are not necessarily the cause of obesity, but they interfere with your ability to stick to a diet. After all, this is the subject with which this book concerns itself the most.

THE LACK OF WILL POWER

As I shall explain later, the use of will power is very inadequate in the control of obesity. As long as you make a conscious effort to stay on a reducing diet, you will lose weight. However, as soon as your mind becomes occupied by other matters, or a new or unexpected crisis arises, you have a tendency to slip back into your previous faulty habit. This compounds your problem because of the added disillusionment and discouragement. Therefore, something more efficient and permanent than will power is needed to enable you to stick to your diet.

Nevertheless, when classifying the psychological causes

of failure in reducing programs, certain types of patients fit this "will power group." I am thinking first of my teen-age patient working behind a soda fountain who found it absolutely impossible to maintain a needed weight loss because of his constant exposure to tasty foods and having to watch other people eating them.

A very successful 38-year-old contractor once said to me, "Now that summer vacation is over and I have lost weight, how can I avoid gaining it back when I do most of my business over the luncheon table?" The individual who transacts much of his business while entertaining his customers with food and drink, finds it extremely difficult to use will power to stick to a diet.

A 40-year-old librarian who has been under my care for a number of years once told me that she had no difficulty in maintaining her proper weight until she was invited to a reception or some other social function where she was exposed to much rich and fattening food, none of which fit in her dietary program. She said, "I could put up with being around food, but when everyone around me is eating, I just can't help myself." Here, again, is a case where a psychologically conditioned set of circumstances tends to cause difficulty.

LACK OF MOTIVATION

Under this heading belong the patients who have tried to diet again and again and who have failed repeatedly. They become so depressed that their psychological mood has been altered to one of complete and utter despair.

Since many of my obesity patients are referred by other physicians, it is not unusual for a patient to say to me "Doctor, I have tried everything and I am so disgusted with myself that I just can't help but eat."

Belonging in the same category is, what I like to label the "I Don't Care" eater. He continues to nibble on highly fattening foods, while all the time he is saying to himself, "This will make me gain, but I don't care—I don't care—I don't care." You, as well as I, know that he *does care*. This is simply a rationalization maintained out of desperation.

FOOD FULFILLS A NEED

Next, we have the compulsive, neurotic eater. If a woman, for instance, she will get along just fine until Mother's Day when her son brings her a box of chocolates. She will put it away in a cupboard because her doctor warned her not to eat sweets. About a week or two later, she will get a strong urge to eat some candy. While no one is watching, she will then take down the box of chocolates. She will first "taste" one piece, then a second, then a third, and so on, until she has eaten the entire contents in a short time. She has a tendency to eat in spurts.

There is a large group of people who feel rejected and insecure and who alleviate their problems by eating. These are the people who have learned to relieve emotional pain by indulging themselves with quantities of tasty and fattening foods. After all, the various mental and emotional anxieties are as disturbing as physical pain. In such cases, food is used as a tranquilizer. As you will see later, you will learn to use nature's own built-in tranquilizer. This should make it unnecessary for you to seek happiness in excessive food or a nerve pill.

The wife of a very successful traveling salesman once told me that the only way she could go to sleep at night was to eat a bedtime snack. Later on, I had a chance to talk to her husband, who was also overweight. He told me that he could go to sleep without eating, but he would always awaken at

2:00 a.m. and would not be able to go back to sleep unless he went to the refrigerator and had a snack. In both instances, these patients were using food as a sedative. Again, it seemed to fulfill a need. This is reminiscent of the infant who does not fall asleep until he has been breast-fed by his mother. It is a childhood trait perpetuated into adulthood.

LACK OF SECURITY AND DEPRESSION

We all know inhibited persons who are afraid to express their emotions. After a trying day of exposure to various anxiety-provoking situations, these people have inhibited their responses so much that they are simmering with repressed emotions. When they finally get home, they eat in order to relieve the tremendous pressure and tension that has built up. They eat large amounts of food, not because they are hungry, but because unconsciously they have learned that it makes them feel better and more secure. Nevertheless, the food that they consume must *taste good*. As I have previously explained, they will not be contented until their taste buds are also satisfied.

There have been many warnings in the medical literature by psychiatrically trained physicians that taking "need-fulfilling" foods away from such persons is poor treatment. They claim that this could precipitate severe depressions. I am in complete disagreement with such a theory and a depression has never occurred in my experience with over 2,000 patients. Remember, we have a built-in release valve; that is, when the patient gets too upset and tense from dieting, he will simply start eating again. Of course, one reason for this tenseness is that he has tried to use will power to overcome his problem. I shall repeatedly inform you in this book that whenever you attempt to change a habit by will power, tension builds up. Therefore, the problem must be approached from a different point of view.

SEXUAL PROBLEMS

The psychoanalysts set forth many theories of overeating, such as the oral-gratification and the sexual-frustration theory. They tell us that food represents a need for love, and that the hunger is really not for food but for love. In certain instances of this type, no doubt psychiatric therapy will be of value, but the large majority of overweight people find that they can get the sexual gratification and love they need much easier when they have a slim, trim figure, rather than when they are unattractive and overweight.

As I have stated before, most of the psychological problems in my obesity patients resolved themselves once they had attained their new figure and maintained it for a sufficiently long period of time. Here, again, the supervision by your personal physician becomes extremely important. Remember, an obese person may develop emotional problems as well as any other person. Eating may then become a crutch for frustrations and anxieties. I used to refer an appreciable number of obese patients to psychiatrists and always tried to examine them a year or two later for a follow-up. I found that many of them had become emotionally stable but almost all of them were still overweight.

I think that by now you can see that I am not attempting to give you a "Do It Yourself" program as the sole solution to your obesity problem. I am simply proposing that in addition to competent professional supervision, *you* must undertake to resolve your problem.

Obesity is one of the few medical conditions where the responsibility of carrying out the program rests with the patient. The purpose of this work is to teach you how you may assume and carry out this responsibility. These methods are in no way meant to serve as a substitute for adequate and proper medical supervision.

Chapter 4

The Responsibility is Yours

Beware of Friends and Supermarkets

THE OBJECTIVES

Up to this point, I have described to you why you have failed in the past. In order to show you how you can be successful in the future, I must first define the four basic objectives that comprise our goal in attaining your proper weight and then in your ability to maintain it.

The objectives are as follows:

1. Motivation.
2. Transference of responsibility to the patient.
3. Realizing the difference between initial and maintenance diet.
4. Methods used to promote adherence to the program.

The main portion of this book will be concerned with the last of these.

MOTIVATION

In order to lose weight, you must be properly motivated. The accusation is often made that the obese person lacks sincerity and does not really try to reduce. The next time one of your thin friends makes this accusation, quote the following statistics: The American public spends over 200 million dollars per year for various liquid diet formulas which are used as food substitutes. Many times I have wondered, in absolute amazement, how some people are able to drink their meals from a can with a straw. If they were not really sincere in losing weight, they certainly would not endure such a dreadful ordeal. Of course, as you well know, this only temporarily controls obesity. No one can live the rest of his life substituting this type of product for food. More than 120 million dollars yearly is spent for drugs and reducing gadgets. Americans also pay over 600 million dollars for girdles and over two million dollars for various types of scales each year. If they did not really care about their obesity, they would not bother to buy these products. Nevertheless, motivation is not strong enough unless an individual can progress from the wishing stage to the action stage. People who spend money in the ways noted above are not considered properly motivated.

Even the threat of death is not enough motivation, as I have discovered in trying to treat some cardiac patients. After recovering from heart attacks, they reduce temporarily, but as soon as they feel the immediate danger is over they resume overeating.

I am sure that at one time or another you have read the statistics about the increase in diabetes, heart disease, coronary disease, infections, arthritis, etc., which is associated with overweight. A person who is 30 percent overweight has an increased mortality rate of 50 percent. These statistics are frightening. Yet, they are not proper inducements to lose weight or maintain the loss because they are all negative motivating factors.

The correct motivation must be positively directed. The reason that you wish to lose weight is because you want to look better, you want to improve your appearance, you want to emerge more attractive and with greater poise and confidence, and you want to feel better, too. Without the burdensome surplus pounds, you will have that feeling of well being — you will be able to participate in sports and devote more time to social and community activities. Your life will become fuller and more enjoyable.

This type of motivation is ego building and is lasting. Therefore, when you undertake the program that I shall outline for you, you must contemplate it, not because you are afraid of certain illnesses or diseases, but because you have a longing to look and feel better. In order to make this program successful, you must accentuate the positive factors. I will talk more about the need for this *positive* attitude later as it will become a very important part of your plan for self-improvement. After all, losing weight is just one aspect of self-improvement.

THE TRANSFERENCE OF RESPONSIBILITY

After your doctor has outlined the proper dietary program that you must follow, it is your responsibility to adhere to it. Accordingly, you must realize that the precepts in this book are aids that you must adopt, and that no one else can do it for you. I will reiterate again and again that until you realize that *you* are the only one who can overcome your weight problem, you are sweeping it under the rug.

To escape self-discipline, many patients subject themselves to all types of uncomfortable treatments, medications, and injections. They listen to all types of gossip and eagerly await every new faddist remedy which will take the responsibility from their shoulders and put it onto some gadget or medication. For this reason, the program that your doctor outlines for you must be one that is as pleasing as possible and acceptable to you. You will not use will power to follow the dietary schedule, but it is always a good idea to make it as pleasing as possible. If you are given an impossible program to follow, it is next to useless to start. There are two big enemies that you will encounter in assuming the responsibility yourself. One is the "monster" supermarket and the second is your "friends." I will discuss them in turn.

THE "MONSTER"

I am referring again to the supermarket. Remember, it is much easier to say "no" in the supermarket than it is at home after you have purchased the fattening food and feel obliged to "use it up."

How often have you seen the following supermarket scene. Mother is pushing the cart down the aisle, little Johnny and Mary are running everywhere and Dad is trailing behind. Mother has her shopping list in front of her and very carefully selects the needed foods from the shelves. While she is doing this, both Johnny and Mary dart back to the cart with all sorts of brightly-colored boxes and packages which they have seen advertised on television. Most of these foods are usually high in carbohydrate content and very fattening. Every so often, Dad also throws something into the cart. By the time Mother gets to the counter, there is a whole group of "surprise" packages in the cart and she is too embarrassed to put them back. She takes them home and is constantly tempted by the new products and invariably trys them all "just to see what they are like."

The other problems are sales and the home freezer. How many times have you bought food in large quantities because it is cheaper during a sale and you can store it in your freezer? You may decide to buy a fattening "treat" food for six months ahead, but unfortunately it is gone in two months. It is too tempting when it is so quickly available.

YOUR "FRIENDS"

It never ceases to amaze me when patients relate how some of their best friends and relatives manifest the most extreme degree of sadism in trying to tempt them to deviate from their diet. Once the diet secret is out, they seem to take inordinate delight in offering them rich and fattening foods. They plead with them to take a second serving or "just taste a little bit." This is very similar to asking an alcoholic to have "just one drink." The downfall of the compulsive eater is just as predictable as that of the alcoholic once he starts getting off his diet.

Many of your friends and relatives may also remark how terrible you look since you have lost weight, thus completely destroying the new slim, attractive image that you are attempting to establish in your mind. Nevertheless, remember that if you maintain your new weight long enough (at least six months), the little wrinkles and looseness of skin usually firm up quite satisfactorily. Most of my patients that have maintained their weight through this initial flabby period appear to be much younger than they were when they started dieting.

Frequently, you will find that your fat friends are your worst enemies. They become very jealous as they see you losing weight and getting a more trim figure. They will try many different ways to minimize your success. They will tell you that you are bound to gain your weight back, that you are not losing enough to matter, that you are losing too fast or that they know of an "easier" method they would like you

37

to try. Remember that the responsibility of carrying out your program is now on your shoulders. Your own doctor has told you what you must do, and you should not let yourself be influenced by other people. Later on, when I teach you to give your subconscious mind the proper suggestions, you must not let other people insinuate the wrong suggestions.

TWO TYPES OF DIETS

Any type of reducing program which ignores the difference between the initial diet and the maintenance diet is doomed to failure. I will go into this in more detail in the last portion of this book. Suffice it to say at this point, the initial diet must be rigid and drastic enough to produce a definite result quickly. If it does not, your initial motivating force to look and feel better will be destroyed. If you cannot see any results, you are not going to continue the program that has been outlined for you. There is nothing that destroys morale (both the patient's and the doctor's) more permanently than a restricted diet that has lasted two months and produced no results.

After you have arrived at your ideal weight, a maintenance program of agreeable, rational, nutritionally sound eating is launched. You may as well realize right now that this maintenance diet will last all your life unless bodily changes indicate otherwise. The person who "just can't wait to get off my diet" will inevitably gain back the weight he lost. His mental attitude has not been properly changed—one of the things I hope to show you how to accomplish by my method.

Once you realize that the two diets are completely different programs, you will understand why your physician must adjust your food lists as you continue under his care.

ADJUNCTIVE AIDS

One way to stick to your diet is by environmental control. For example, you could go into a hospital and be sure you would be served only indicated food.

Dr. Garfield G. Duncan of Pennsylvania Hospital in Philadelphia has very successfully treated a series of "intractable" cases by what he terms "periodic starvation." The patient is placed in the hospital for two weeks and is given nothing to eat except fluids such as tea and water. He is also given some vitamin supplements. After the first 24 to 48 hours, because of a chemical change in the blood, the patient loses his hunger and can continue the abstinence without difficulty. At the end of two weeks, most patients showed a weight loss of 25 pounds. They are subsequently placed on a maintenance diet.

The interesting thing about this program is that most patients are then able to stick to a restricted diet much easier. As one such patient remarked to me, "You know, doctor, the portions that I am allowed to eat now look so much bigger to me than they did before." What actually has been accomplished is that the patient's image of himself and his requirements for food have become more realistic.

Of course, your own personal physician must decide whether this regimen is suitable for your case. However, I shall show you later how this image of yourself and your dietary needs can be changed without resorting to such drastic measures.

Another way to control the environment would be to have you live at a sanatorium or one of the so-called "reducing farms," but these plans, like the hospital plan, are not financially practical and you must always return to your permanent environment anyway.

DRUG THERAPY

Another way to adhere to your diet is by the use of certain drugs. In some instances, your doctor may prescribe some glandular extract such as pituitary or thyroid. These hormones, however, have no direct effect on your ability to stick to a diet, and their use is not within the scope of this book, but depends upon the professional judgment of your personal physician.

On the other hand, a large group of drugs called anorexiants lift your mood and make you feel satisfied with less food. Even so, many of them have unpleasant side reactions and you cannot stay on them indefinitely. Despite this, I do not object to using these medications, especially initially, when you are first learning the techniques in this book.

During an experiment with 50 volunteers at the School of Aerospace Medicine, Dr. Paul Musgrave noted an interesting finding. His volunteers were placed on 350 calories a day and were given one of the appetite-spoiling drugs. They lost an average of three and a half pounds a week. The peculiar effect he noted was that only those who cheated on their 350-calorie diet complained of side effects from these drugs. The ones who did not cheat seemed to have no difficulty. There is, at this time, no known pharmacological explanation for the relationship between tolerance to these drugs and caloric intake. More work along this line is being done at present.

Other drugs such as diuretics (causing an increased flow of urine), bulk producers and cathartics are of no value in removal of adipose tissue. Tranquilizers are occasionally of temporary value, but should be avoided for extended intervals because of a tendency to develop dependence on them.

MOOD ALTERATION

There are, as has been stated, many drugs that elevate the mood, but the best and most permanent way to alter your negative feelings about dieting is to program only positive and constructive thoughts into your mind. Unfortunately, as my extensive library on overweight proves, almost everything that has been written about losing weight dwells on the difficulties one will encounter. After a bout with the literature on obesity, most people feel they are beaten before they start.

These negative comments on reducing, added to any memories of previous frustrated attempts at dieting, have been penetrating your subconscious mind for so long that drastic counter measures must be adopted to eliminate their effect on your attitude. They have become so ingrained that many people say, "I just can't seem to lose weight" with an air of pride as though this were an accomplishment. Recognize this for what it is—a rationalization or face saving device which gives you an excuse not to do something about a serious problem.

It is true that some individuals, because of inherited body structure, will normally weigh more than others, but gross overweight is not normal for anybody and the sooner you realize this the sooner you will be on the way to better appearance and better health.

CHEWING THE FAT

One way to alter your feelings about reducing is through group therapy or what I like to refer to as, "Chewing the Fat" therapy. The success of this approach is shown by the numerous TOPS (Take Off Pounds Sensibly) clubs, which have sprung up all over the United States. There are several ways that group therapy alters the mood and exerts a beneficial effect. In a group, you see other patients with the same problem, most of them losing weight. They are relaxed and happy about their progress, and this has a favorable influence on your mood, since it counteracts the previously described "insurmountable difficulties" attitude. Likewise, the fact that there are people who are interested in you and are watching you closely, at weekly intervals, has a tendency to alter any feelings of loneliness and despair. This is closely coupled with the competitive spirit often manifested at such group meetings. I am strongly in favor of these clubs and would recommend them very highly to all patients with an obesity problem. This organization can exert a tremendously powerful, positive, suggestive influence on your conscious and subconscious mind. You can locate the closest group in your city by writing to the national headquarters, TOPS Club, Inc., 3180 S. 27th Street, Milwaukee 15, Wisconsin.

Nevertheless, difficulties can develop within such a group. Some patients may feel that they are different from the rest, and that the principles discussed at these meetings do not apply to them. This again has a negative influence and they need supplementary help. This supplementary help must come from directed self-conditioning, specifically medical self-hypnosis. We will go into that after further discussion of some things you should know before attempting self-hypnosis.

Chapter 5

You Must Change Your Attitude

Accentuate the Positive

GET IN THE RIGHT MOOD

I have shown you in the last chapter that the secret of sticking to a diet is to change your negative attitude to a positive one that will prevent you from becoming discouraged or depressed and insure your success. You have been told that learning to carry out a diet effortlessly involves utilizing the same psychological principles you employ in mastering any new skill. If you are not even able to *imagine* that you are going to be successful, then you are defeated before you begin. This is exactly what happens when you undertake a reducing diet with a pervading sense of failure resulting from your inability to follow previous diets, and a premonition that you will be unequal to the task again.

Remember, I told you that no amount of will power can surmount this feeling of defeatism, and whenever you attempt to pit will power against a bad habit, you eventually become so tense that your efforts fail and the bad habit remains.

I am assuming that you have a genuine desire to start on a reducing program and follow it as long as necessary. It may be that you have been putting off starting such a program and that you are still waiting to "get into the mood." You can probably find all sorts of excuses why you wish to postpone such a project. Your first step is to stop deceiving yourself. Avoiding a problem does not solve it, and only strengthens your feeling of inadequacy. You must develop feelings of self-esteem and confidence. You must cultivate a feeling that you will be successful in dieting just as you would have to develop a feeling that you could accomplish any task you undertook. In other words, you must start to develop a positive self-image.

A superficial attempt to undertake a diet is not enough. Your self-image must be truly changed by appropriate suggestions given to yourself, and you must make strong efforts to make these suggestions a permanent part of your drive to succeed in dieting and any other problems you may have.

STOP GIVING YOURSELF NEGATIVE SUGGESTIONS

To understand how *positive* suggestions will help you to stick to your diet, you must first understand how *negative* suggestions and continual downgrading of yourself have prevented you from realizing your goal in the past. For example, you have probably said many times, "I just can't seem to lose weight," or "I was born to be fat." Undoubtedly, you have also said that there is no use dieting because "I will gain my weight back as soon as I stop taking these pills and start eating again." You have repeated these statements so often you have convinced yourself that they are true.

These assertions are usually based on past memories of failure so they are true to some extent. On the other hand, you must recognize that the constant repetition of negative suggestions has increased your sense of futility. Unfortunately, all these negative opinions, true or not, filter into your subconscious mind which does not question or analyze the many impressions that it receives. You have incessantly presented negative suggestions about yourself to your subconscious mind, and this has finally had such a strong effect on your conscious activity that you have lost all power for positive, constructive action.

YOUR SELF-IMAGE

You should realize by now that the image you have of yourself—both of your personality and body—determines to a large extent how you will go about solving the various problems you face. If you have attempted to lose weight before and failed repeatedly, your total image of yourself ultimately becomes established and fixed. You become so convinced that you are incapable of the strength necessary to begin and maintain a diet that you eventually stop mentally picturing an attractive body image. It is too frustrating and depressing to look at this image so you resign yourself to your unattractive appearance and indulge in rationalizations.

To illustrate how important your self-image is, let us go back to your childhood days. You will remember that you always got the highest marks in the subject you liked the most. At the same time, you probably received the poorest grade in the one you disliked the most. It should be clear that your positive attitude helped you obtain the good grades in the course you liked. You had more confidence in yourself. You were certain that you would be successful and that it would be easy for you. It is this self-confidence which will be generated by the proper self-image. Once you have the conviction of being able to stick to your diet, you can carry it out easily. Therefore, your basic problem is one of changing your psychological mood.

I am not telling you to deceive yourself by arbitrarily stating that you are more confident, and that repetition of the statement will make it so and automatically insure the success of your diet. Positive attitudes must be fed into your subconscious mind without being evaluated by the critical factor of your conscious intellect. The most effective way you can counteract negative feelings and establish positive beliefs is in a state of self-hypnosis. You might ask at this point, "How can I possibly imagine myself reducing successfully when it is something that I have never been able to do?" Be that as it may, remember that every successful person has had to be capable of visualizing himself as a success long before it became a reality. A physician, for example, could not possibly undertake the many years of study and self-deprivation a medical degree requires unless he was first able to see himself, in his mind's eye as some day being successful and a help to mankind. Consequently, you cannot possibly expect to lose weight successfully and attain a slim, trim figure unless you are able to "see" yourself achieving this result in your imagination.

Many obstacles may arise during your reducing program. But when you are able to envision yourself as trim and attractive, these obstacles, instead of becoming road blocks, will become stepping stones to success. Remember that difficulties can either strengthen or weaken your ability to meet challenges. You can ask any successful person and they will tell you that the only way they were able to reach their goal was by overcoming handicaps which defeated people who were less motivated.

YOUR SUBCONSCIOUS IS A GOAL-STRIVING MECHANISM

The subconscious part of your mind (which contains your memory) can be compared to a computer. It is continually being furnished with data from the conscious part of your mind. It cannot change these data, but it can send them back to the conscious part of your mind for conscious action. This process can be compared with the modern programming of electronic computers. The computer cannot change the material it is given but it can coordinate all factors of a problem and furnish instantaneous answers.

The subconscious mind of the human brain is analogous to a goal-striving computer or, as it is called, a servo-mechanism. For example, in learning to play the piano, you feed various specific data into your subconscious mind. You supply it with detailed information, indicating which finger depresses what key in response to reading certain printed notes. Eventually, after your hands automatically respond to the visual stimulus of notes, you do not have to think about where you place each finger for each note. Your subconscious mind automatically directs the movements of your fingers as your conscious mind reads the notes. In other words, you have provided your subconscious mind with a series of data which it memorizes and can furnish to the conscious mind when it needs this information and recall to reach a predetermined goal.

Now let us carry this one step further. Suppose you want to play a musical selection from memory rather than from the impulses of notes. You first program the series of notes into your subconscious mind in an orderly manner, and once they have been integrated into the subconscious you can reproduce them without any conscious effort. Your subconscious mind now guides you, not in response to immediate visual impulses but from remote visual impulses that have been stored as part of your memory. When something has been learned in this way, it can be executed while your conscious mind is engaged in other activity. For example, a well-trained professional pianist can be discussing an entirely unrelated topic with another person while he correctly plays a musical selection, at least as far as the notes are concerned. The behavior of his fingers has been completely taken over by the subconscious mind.

This is comparable to the obese person who automatically eats a whole box of candy while watching television. At the end of the evening he is surprised to find there are no chocolates left. Consciously, he is completely unaware of the behavior of his fingers, mouth, chewing, and swallowing because these functions are taken over by the subconscious mind. Consciously, he is thinking only of the entertainment but his subconscious mind, previously trained to carry out this harmful behavior pattern through repeated episodes of eating candy while relaxing and watching television, continues to follow the program it has learned. Most individuals seek to stop this habit by conscious effort and will power, but it would be much better to program a new habit pattern into the subconscious mind until it became a strong conditioned reflex incapable of error.

Before I describe the details of such a technique, however, you must understand more about the actual process of "feeding" the subconscious mind. Therefore, let us return to our example of learning to play the piano.

POSITIVE AND NEGATIVE FEEDBACK

The intricacies of piano playing are first performed haltingly by the conscious mind but as proficiency increases the subconscious mind memorizes the correct sequence of notes and even the mood of the music. From that time on, the subconscious automatically corrects mistakes. This is analogous to an electronically guided missile which, the moment it steers off course, feeds back data to the electronic brain (the computer mechanism) that error has occurred. The correct course is then communicated back to the missile which veers back on target again. This is what is sometimes referred to as negative feedback. As soon as the missile corrects its path, it informs the electronic brain that it is again on course. This is referred to as positive feedback. This same process occurs in the human brain as you are learning to play the piano. Every time you make an error, it is corrected by negative feedback. As soon as you are playing correctly, it is maintained by positive feedback. Eventually, the right memory pattern becomes dominant and negative feedback is seldom needed.

THE SUBCONSCIOUS IS AN AUTOMATIC MECHANISM

If I were to ask you to eat a spoonful of ice cream, you would probably comply, paying no attention to the number of muscles and memories required to raise the ice cream from dish to mouth. Your subconscious mind automatically controls every detail of the activity—the picking up of the spoon, moving it towards the dish of ice cream, cutting into the ice cream with the spoon, gathering up a portion of it, directing the spoon to your mouth, drawing the ice cream off the spoon with your lips, propelling it to the back of your tongue, finally swallowing it, and then returning the spoon to the dish. Eating a spoonful of ice cream seems simple, yet infants can and do make a mess out of this simple act before it has been memorized by the subconscious.

The infant will move the spoon erratically, perhaps drop it a few times, and may even miss his mouth repeatedly. After many attempts, he finally succeeds by repeated negative feedback which has been conveyed to his subconscious mind. When, at last, he has performed the maneuver successfully, it is stored as a permanent pattern of the subconscious. Thereafter it is "remembered" correctly by the subconscious mind and the infant performs the motions without mistakes.

FEEDING YOUR SUBCONSCIOUS MIND

Now that you appreciate that the subconscious mind is both a goal-striving and an automatic mechanism at the same time, I will briefly outline the principle of using this mechanism in changing your eating habits. I will later go into much more detail of exact methods. At this point, I want you to grasp only the theory that underlies the methods.

The theory, of course, is that the subconscious mind is automatically going to guarantee your success in following a diet if it is given the proper information and suggestions. The subconscious mind has proved time and again that it can make no error if it is programmed correctly. To implement the theory, you must visualize yourself exactly as you wish to be. This means you must "see" your body as it should be and recognize the program that will result in this goal. You must then experience, in your mind, the feeling that you will have while you are actually carrying out your diet.

As you begin to lose weight, you must seek constantly to reinforce the new habit patterns and mental pictures of your success. Strictly speaking, you will be establishing a new conditioned response, as I mentioned earlier. We will discuss these responses more fully in the next chapter.

Once you achieve the ultimate results from using your subconscious mind, the maintenance of your weight will become effortless. Your built-in guidance system will be working perfectly. When something interferes with the proper functioning of your subconscious mind, it will recognize the error immediately and it will be corrected by the feedback mechanism. This negative feedback is not the same as negative thoughts, which I previously discussed. The former is helpful because it helps you correct the situation, whereas the latter is just the opposite and influences you in a harmful way.

Your initial efforts in using your subconscious mind will require a certain amount of "mental set" (or anticipation) which will encompass all your goals and aspirations. However, if you will practice this technique daily, the results that you have been seeking will occur spontaneously. It is true that you will, at first, require a certain amount of mental discipline, but this will involve learning to program thoughts into your subconscious mind, not will power.

Once a favorable response pattern has been established, the subconscious mind will automatically guide you toward the end you are pursuing. You will simply be giving the "command" to stick to your diet, and your subconscious mind will translate this into actions which insure the results you are seeking. This, again, is very similar to the pianist who commands his fingers to play certain notes. You will be responding to a learned and remembered pattern which you have previously programmed into your subconscious mind.

YOU HAVE DONE IT BEFORE

It is possible you may think that the methods suggested are too difficult but if you think about it for a moment you will realize that you have been using similar methods for years. For example, if you knew that three months from now you were going to take a vacation, you would immediately start thinking of all the pleasant things you would do. These anticipatory emotions have an uplifting effect on your entire being. When your vacation really begins, you will have established a "mental set" or outline for enjoying the occasion. Consequently, you will instinctively do the many things that you have already visualized in your mind weeks before you actually left on your trip.

If you do not look forward to a certain event, the emotions and mental pictures can have the opposite effect. For instance, if you start worrying weeks ahead about having to attend a certain social function, imagining all the embarrassing, irksome and uncomfortable situations you might get into, you are certain to dislike the event. Your mental set is such that you will, in fact, develop all the unfavorable reactions that you imagined.

Perhaps these two examples of "anticipation" will help you see how you have sold yourself on the idea you could not diet. Your fears that you would always overeat at a banquet are always corroborated by the fact that you do. On the other hand, if you have furnished your subconscious mind with information of a positive nature, such as your ability to restrain yourself, you would behave correctly since you had not imagined yourself behaving any other way.

It must be clear that your imagination must create a new mental image of yourself. Right now, after you read this paragraph, put down this book and try to picture yourself looking trim and attractive, as well as very pleased with yourself. If you will dwell on this image for a few moments, you should very soon begin to notice a general feeling of well-being and accomplishment. It may be only momentary at present, but it is the feeling that can guide you to your goal. You will be able to feel this sense of confidence for prolonged periods with more practice.

WILL POWER IS NOT THE ANSWER

You will notice throughout this chapter that I have stressed the use of the imagination rather than the use of will power.

If you had been successful using your will power, you probably would not be reading this book. Obviously, it did not work the way you wanted it to work, and you realize that you require something more. You recognize now that the fallacy in using will power is that you are consciously putting too much emphasis on your previous failures. As a result, your mental set is not conducive to improvement and efforts prove only more frustrating. Success in using this visual imagery depends upon your subconscious mind's uncritical acceptance of constructive suggestions. The method of achieving this will be by the use of self-hypnosis, a technique that you will need to practice every day in order to gain results.

As you experience making headway in your attempt to reduce, you will automatically get the "feel" of losing weight easily and pleasurably. This feeling can be compounded by continued success until you reach a satisfactory conclusion. This is very similar to an experience with which you are probably familiar. Take the example of a basketball team which has been playing poorly. Suddenly, the team starts making a few points and unexpectedly gets "hot." The players start to score basket after basket. Some people would call this a "lucky streak." Actually, it is nothing more than a compounding of success, each success bringing more success. This is simply one manifestation of what I have been describing in this chapter and the technique you will use to lose, control, and maintain your correct weight.

Chapter 6

How Poor Eating Habits Are Formed

Calling Doctor Pavlov

DOCTOR PAVLOV'S DOGS

From time to time in these pages I have referred variously to a psychological process which can be utilized to produce permanent physiological changes through "burying" faulty habit and eating patterns (negative) under layers of new habit patterns (positive) constructed to help the overweight individual visualize himself at his correct weight, reduce to that weight, and then maintain it.

Conditioned or automatic reflexes, conditioned or automatic responses and results obtained with a minimum of conscious effort are some of the ways this process is termed, and it is not new. What is new is the merger of this process with hypnosis and/or self-hypnosis to potentiate its value.

The most common name for this potent process is conditioned reflexology, and its therapeutic use to aid humans evolved from a series of fascinating experiments performed by Ivan Pavlov, a renowned Russian physiologist and physician (1849-1936) who used dogs in his first investigations. His research is now the basis of Russian psychiatry along with its powerful adjunct—hypnosis. Dr. Pavlov's most famous experiment was one in which he rang a bell just before he gave a dog some food. After many such "bell-food" presentations, he then began to ring the bell without supplying the food. The dog reacted to the bell with an increased flow of saliva, licking of his chops, and an eagerness that indicated he was acting exactly as he would have if food were in front of him. Repeated exposures to the bell and subsequent food had conditioned him to associate the bell with food.

Dr. Pavlov performed hundreds of similar experiments to prove that frustration, depression, neurosis and other harmful symptoms could be produced by variations of his first conditioning process. They are too numerous to mention here but the thing to remember is that his methods can be employed to help you in your fight against overweight.

TELEVISION IS A BELL

It should be easy for you to recognize the importance of Dr. Pavlov's work because you have, during your lifetime, conditioned yourself to all sorts of "bells" compelling you to eat or develop a desire for food. This is a conditioned response which has become automatic, and in your case it has been negative conditioning. Any type of situation may be the bell. For example, supposing that year after year you have become accustomed to eating a snack while watching television, constantly associating the watching of television with food. Eventually, whenever you turn on the television, you automatically go to the refrigerator and get a snack. The bell (watching television) has caused a conditioned response (snacking) and your conscious mind is little involved in perpetuating the harmful habit.

An even more familiar example is your response to television commercials picturing tempting arrays of food. When combined with mouth-watering descriptions by the announcer your salivary glands go to work and you become unbearably hungry. Your conditioned response provokes your appetite and an increased flow of saliva just as with Pavlov's dogs. You have become conditioned to respond to pictures and words about food and your trip to the refrigerator is compulsive and predictable. Your predictability is the reason sponsors advertise.

FOOD AS A PACIFIER

There are many such examples in the life of the average obese person which result in overindulgence and poor eating habits. Some of these habits go back to childhood when infants are given the breast or formula no matter what is causing its distress. Food and comfort become inextricably intertwined and is used as a pacifier.

Individuals who carry childhood patterns built around food into their adult life usually become obese. They become so habituated to using food to allay tension, anxiety, pain, frustration and other emotional symptoms that eventually they attempt to solve all their "unbearable" problems in this way. Here are some examples:

Little three-year-old Mary falls and hurts her knee. She comes to mother. Mother gives her a piece of candy and "makes it well." (Mother is the greatest doctor in the world.) Candy becomes associated with the soothing of pain.

Little five-year-old Johnny doesn't finish eating his vegetables. Mother and daddy bribe Johnny by telling him that he can have cake if he "cleans his plate." This is a painful situation for Johnny, but he soon learns that tasty foods enable him to endure unpleasant circumstances, both physical and mental.

While I am on the subject, I might also mention that conditioning a child to clean the plate is often an important contributory factor to obesity in adult life. Many obese persons automatically eat everything set before them—even though they already feel full—just to clean the plate. They have been conditioned to feel uncomfortable unless they finish all the food on the platter. I will have more to say about this in the chapter on specific techniques of self-hypnosis for reducing.

FOOD AS A REWARD

Many people who do not use food to appease emotional symptoms become nearly as much a slave to food by using it as a reward. This, too, starts in childhood when parents reward their children with treats for work well done at school and in the home or for good behavior. In adult life they will reward themselves with food for a good day's work, a promotion, getting a new customer and a variety of other things. Soon they are rewarding themselves at the slightest provocation and the battle of the bulge has begun. To illustrate this mechanism the following typical conditioning process is cited:

Bill is 15 years old and is on his way to meet his first date, Jackie. He is making a little money doing gardening on weekends. On his way over to Jackie's house, he stops to buy a large box of chocolates. Meeting her at the door, he presents it to her. Food has become a symbol of reward to both Bill and Jackie.

Fifteen years later Bill and Jackie, now married, have

three children of their own. By this time they are both a little on the stout side, but today they are celebrating their 10th wedding anniversary. How are they going to celebrate? They are going to go to the most expensive restaurant in town for a big dinner; and, of course, when it is time for dessert, they will order a rich strawberry short cake. Even though they are both full, it is included in the price of the meal and they feel it would be a shame to "waste food,"— ("remember to clean your plate" — "don't waste food") and "besides it is our wedding anniversary." As a matter of course, they eat it. Can you see how they had been conditioned to clean the plate and to use food as a reward?

THE ROLE OF BOREDOM

Motives for overeating vary greatly and in many cases stem from diametrically opposite life situations. Thus, the high-strung actor, singer or business executive uses food as a form of relaxation while housewives "raid the icebox" to add a festive note to the monotony of their work. The factor of boredom cannot be too strongly emphasized. Every physician is familiar with the patient who confesses he has no particular craving for food but just eats "for something to do." Such patients admit they eat even when they have little or no appetite. Labor saving devices and "quick" foods have given modern man a great deal of leisure time, but he has not learned to utilize it and boredom is one of the badges of our society.

HOW HABITS BECOME ESTABLISHED

You have conditioned yourself to one, some, or all of the foregoing neurotic eating habits by constant repetition. You have, in other words, been reacting as automatically as Pavlov's famous dogs. You have eaten so much of the wrong foods for so long that the whole procedure has become compulsive and involuntary. In other words, the habits have become established through a learning process. What you may not realize, however, is the power of such an established habit. Consider the following illustration from every day experience.

Suppose that during the past year, in going to work every morning, you drive down Adams Boulevard, past 10th Avenue and to 20th Avenue, where you turn left to reach your office.

One morning as you get into your car, you decide to turn left on 10th Avenue. After you are on your way, you may be intensely engaged in an interesting conversation or you may be meditating about a difficult unrelated problem. In such an instance, your habit pattern may cause you to drive right on past 10th Avenue and make your usual left turn on to 20th Avenue. You may not realize what you have done until you reach your office. The only way to stop the repetition of an established habit is to give it your continuous conscious attention, unless, of course, you use the methods I outline for you in this book.

The wrong eating habits, once established, are just as powerful. Attempting to break them through the use of will power requires a constant conscious effort. The difficulty with this method is that the effort may be relaxed at the first serious crisis. Since you can only think about one thing at a time under stress, your conscious mind becomes occupied with other problems and the old habits return. How many times have you gone on a reducing diet using will power to control your poor habits? Then suddenly, someone close to you, a member of your family or intimate friend, becomes ill and you have to take him to the hospital. While anxiously awaiting the doctor there, you go down to the coffee shop to eat. In all likelihood you will order something that tastes good, probably a high carbohydrate or fattening food. While you are eating, you are not even thinking about your diet. You are so concerned about your friend and your mind is so occupied with his illness that you have no time to make a conscious effort to use will power to counteract old bad habits. You unwittingly slip back to your previous tendencies of eating the wrong foods. This is the reason why reducing diets which are based on mere use of will power will ultimately end in failure.

It is far better to change your wrong habit patterns through the same process by which they became established. That is to say, you must "unlearn" the old and "learn" the new proper food habits.

In addition to relearning how to eat, you must learn to handle all the tensions and frustrations of daily existence in an adult manner, and that means without depending on fattening foods. This will not be easy at first but it is a well-known psychological axiom that a strong emotion can always supplant a weaker one, and if you truly want to lose weight and maintain your loss you can do it.

You can count on the conditioned reflex to aid you. Indeed, it will do the work for you after you have learned to program the correct thoughts and pictures into your subconscious mind. Very soon you will find your new habit patterns crowding out the old, and the process will become faster and easier as time goes on.

WHY MEDICAL HYPNOSIS?

Your greatest aid will be hypnosis or self-hypnosis. In this state of mind the road to the subconscious is open with none of the blocks common to the ordinary waking state to bar the flow of mental pictures and processes you wish to instill in your memory permanently.

After studying the fitful dieting of those who attempt to lose weight through will power alone, it becomes clear that hypnosis is the only sensible way to maintain your correct weight. Ideally, you should employ the services of a physician who is competent in the use of medical hypnosis. However, you would soon discover that all hypnosis is merely another form of self-hypnosis. Hence, after learning the techniques of self-hypnosis, you will be able to enter this state and give yourself the necessary constructive suggestions. If you are able to find a physician who can teach you to go into the state initially, I strongly urge you to do so.

The material that I shall present to you, in subsequent chapters, will help you to continue the program that your physician will start for you and enable you to carry it to its natural conclusion.

Chapter 7

Self-Hypnosis is the Answer

You Are Hypnotized Every Day

WHAT IS MEDICAL HYPNOSIS?

Hypnosis has been defined in many ways but most investigators believe it is a state of mind associated with heightened suggestibility in which the subject is able, uncritically, to accept ideas for self-improvement and then act on them appropriately. It is a natural and normal phenomenon of everyday life and it goes back, under one label or another, to antiquity. More than 3,000 years ago, Egyptian priests were using procedures similar to those in practice today, and the cures which occurred in their "sleep temples" were attributed to the trance-like states attained by their subjects.

We know today, of course, that hypnosis is not sleep, nor is it unconsciousness or even a trance although, to an onlooker, a hypnotized subject may appear to be in one of these states. Actually, hypnosis is just the opposite of sleep and subjects, even though their eyes are closed, are in a state of super-awareness. The suggestions of the hypnotherapist, if they are in accord with the predetermined wishes of the subject, are transmitted directly to the subconscious mind which permanently records everything in millions of memory cells. Nevertheless, the subject retains complete possession of his faculties and may reject suggestions which are contrary to his moral principles.

There is nothing mystical or supernatural about hypnosis, though many people apparently believe it consists of a series of "magical gestures" which can cure them in much the same way witch doctors used to cure their patients. Many others, despite a wealth of medical and psychological evidence to the contrary, apparently believe all the potent results attributed to hypnosis are part of a gigantic hoax.

NOT A PANACEA

The truth, as usual, lies somewhere between these extremes. The hypnotherapist *does* use a ritual of one kind or another to induce hypnosis, but he uses it merely to facilitate the subjects entering into this state of mind. *He does not put the subject under but "guides him" into hypnosis.* The therapist acts as a teacher, and the subject always retains complete selectivity as to which suggestions he will accept.

Far from being a hoax, hypnosis has been used to assist in childbirth, still the unbearable pain of terminal cancer, act as an anesthesia when a patient cannot tolerate drugs and alleviate the symptoms of a variety of psychosomatic complaints. On the other hand, it is not a panacea, and cannot be expected to cure all the ills of mankind, although it may be of inestimable value when properly utilized by competent professional men and used in conjunction with other therapeutic methods. Physicians, dentists and psychologists look upon it as just another tool in their fight against human misery, and no ethical member of these professions would ever say it is a specific cure for anything. Nevertheless, it is a powerful aid in many of their procedures.

MISCONCEPTIONS ABOUT HYPNOSIS

Despite the fact hypnosis is used routinely today, many people have misconceptions about its nature and use. A large group, for instance, thinks hypnosis weakens the will, is most easily achieved by not-so-bright individuals, and that the subject can be forced to obey the suggestions of the hypnotherapist. The truth is exactly the opposite of these opinions. As you will see later, it has nothing to do with will power, but is made effective by stimulation of the imagination. Since good communication between hypnotist and subject is essential, intelligence is actually an advantage rather than a hindrance.

Additionally, those who have been hypnotized hundreds of times show an amazing increase in will power. They will themselves, with the help of their imaginations, to become proficient in many endeavors in which they had previously failed.

There are other misconceptions but all of them are based on fear of the unknown and have no foundation in fact.

YOU ARE HYPNOTIZED EVERY DAY

I have stated that hypnosis is a part of everyday life. I will go even further and state we are all hypnotized to some extent every day. If a radio or television commercial suggests you purchase a certain commodity and you act upon this suggestion (as we all do at one time or another) you have let your heightened state of suggestibility lead you into a form of hypnotic behavior, and no one recognizes this better than advertisers.

Here is another example that many of my women readers

will attest to. You have just acquired a new dress or hair-do, and someone whose judgment you value greatly will say, "Your hair-do just doesn't look right." Or he may simply give you a questioning glance when first noticing a new dress you are wearing, without making any remarks whatever, giving you a non-verbal suggestion that something about your dress just "doesn't seem right."

Very likely you begin to wonder about your choice. Before long, you will feel that your dress is too long, too short, too small, too big, or that it bulges or doesn't bulge in the right or wrong places. Chances are that the longer you wear this dress, the more unhappy you become with it. Sooner or later, you will find some excuse for discarding it, such as "I never did like that dress anyway."

In this instance, you have minimized your own ability to judge how it looks on you and substituted another person's unspoken opinion. In other words, you have "locked your mind" around the specific idea, and you act accordingly by getting rid of the dress.

HYPNOSIS IS LEARNED

Although you can enter into a state of hypnosis spontaneously, it is, in the main, a learned accomplishment. One reason it must be learned is because most of the ideas laymen have about hypnosis are erroneous. Since fear is the one big enemy of this state, you must first "unlearn" the popular misconceptions and misgivings regarding this subject. But you can recognize that unlearning is also learning inasmuch as it is a process in which you substitute correct information for incorrect information.

One of the things you must learn is that hypnosis is part of the communication process, and you must closely follow the directions of the hypnotherapist which have been chosen for their impact on your imagination. In self-hypnosis you must follow instructions similar to ones that I will give you in the next chapter.

The two most important things you must learn to use in seeking the hypnotic state are your ability to focus your attention and your imagination. Focusing your attention on a specific idea is a conditioned function (there's Pavlov again) but imagination, in varying degrees, is common to everybody. Nevertheless, the imagination can be enhanced by constant practice, letting the mind's eye dwell on helpful thoughts and images.

You must also cultivate motivation to facilitate hypnosis because you only defeat yourself if you take a negative attitude toward this subject. Proper motivation and expectancy results in the conviction that you *will* enter hypnosis, and conviction of hypnosis *is* hypnosis. Dr. William S. Kroger, who wrote the foreword for this book, has a definition of hypnosis which sums up this idea clearly and concisely. "Hypnosis results," he states, "when faith, hope, confidence and expectation are all catalyzed by the imagination."

YOU MUST BE WILLING

There it is in a nutshell. I would only add that it is voluntary and actually self-induced — a consent state. You cannot be hypnotized against your will. You actually hypnotize yourself. The experienced hypnotist with an extensive knowledge of this subject merely shows you how you can accomplish this. By following his directions you are able to achieve hypnosis—granted you are willing to do so. Some persons who have watched stage hypnotists at work are persuaded otherwise, but the very fact that the subject appears on the stage when volunteers are called for indicates he has given consent. He has given consent, he is willing and expects to be hypnotized and he *will* be hypnotized.

Under the proper circumstances almost anyone can be hypnotized as long as communication can be established and fear eliminated. A very few individuals have personality traits which preclude their becoming hypnotized unless they change certain attitudes. These include the inability to have faith in anything, excessive cynicism, being too analytical and intellectualizing what is basically an emotional experience.

It should be added here that hypnosis is a most pleasant experience. Although you are deeply relaxed and comfortable, you are acutely aware of everything that is being said. In hypnosis, the "critical factor" of the conscious mind is by-passed and the suggestions are stored as memories in the subconscious where they eventually, after few or many repetitions, become that part of your knowledge that operates automatically to help solve your problems. The critical factor stems from that part of your mind which uses logic to evaluate incoming stimuli.

Actors and actresses who have difficulty in memorizing their lines recognize the learning process implicit in hypnosis and use it to master long and difficult dialogue. Students also utilize hypnosis to aid them in remembering involved academic subjects.

THAT REFLEX AGAIN

The conditioned reflex is the basis of successful hypnotherapy. It operates from the very start. For instance, if you accept the hypnotherapist's first suggestion, you will accept each succeeding suggestion more quickly and utilize it more efficiently. This compounding of suggestions leads ultimately to the conviction of hypnosis. You are convinced you are hypnotized because you find you are following the suggestions hypnotically and posthypnotically without conscious volition. Most of you probably know that a suggestion that is acted on later, when out of hypnosis, is a posthypnotic response.

The theory of the conditioned reflex is that it becomes stronger and stronger, and the theory is perfectly proved by hypnosis. Properly and constantly conditioned to avoid certain fattening foods, you would eventually find it easy to abstain from eating them.

IMAGINATION IS THE KEY

I must emphasize that none of the methods I outline will prove too difficult if you allow full reign to your imagination. Will power, as I have stated, is never as powerful as imagination, and when the two come into conflict the latter always wins.

Consider one of the negative aspects of the imagination, for example. You will agree with me that walking across a plank one foot wide and 20 feet long would be a simple feat. But suppose that same plank stretched between two points 150 feet in the air. Again I think you will agree that few people would care to walk across it. Why? Their imaginations conjure up a vivid picture of themselves precariously trying to maintain their balance and finally plunging to the ground. No amount of will power could make them try this feat.

On the other hand, consider the high steel construction men who walk along girders 50 stories up in the air. If you talk to them you will find they can do this because they have conditioned themselves to thinking of this feat as little different than walking across the same girder on the ground. It seems impossible to most of us but they have been conditioned to a different set of circumstances, and they have used their imaginations to help, not hinder them.

Another point you may learn from the above illustration is that whenever you attempt to pit will power against imagination, tension develops since the latter is the stronger. In trying to diet using will power to overcome your improper images of previous failure you become so tense that often you will eventually give up. Nevertheless, if you first change this image to one of success and then go on a diet, this tension is eliminated and you achieve your goal.

Remember that you are being constantly exposed to anxiety-provoking food situations in our modern society. When the tension builds to a sufficiently high level, a safety valve mechanism takes place and you relieve the nervousness by eating. Thus, you can readily understand that there are really two reasons why will power fails in the life long project of a reducing program. They are as follows:

The first reason is the *SUBCONSCIOUS MECHANISM.* You relax conscious effort because your mind becomes occupied with other matters and you slip back to your previous poor eating patterns.

Second is the *CONSCIOUS MECHANISM.* In spite of conscious vigilance, the battle between habit and will power, with its resultant anxiety, initiates the above described safety valve mechanism. Since, in this instance, the obese patient is completely aware of his dietary indiscretion, he will usually rationalize his blunder by saying, "Oh, the heck with the diet!" or, "I don't really care—I'm just too nervous to diet!"

CONSCIOUS AND SUBCONSCIOUS

As you have seen throughout this book, I have been talking about the conscious mind and the subconscious mind.

The term "unconscious mind" would actually be a better one, but I avoid its use because many readers might get the mistaken notion that the procedures outlined would have to be learned in a state of unconsciousness. Since this is one of the major misconceptions about hypnosis and it is obviously impossible to teach anything to someone who is unconscious, I elect not to use the word.

The word subconscious means different things to different people. Therefore, I must define what I mean when I use it. Whenever you see this word in these pages you may assume that I am speaking of the deeper mind—the one below the level of consciousness.

Visualize the picture of an iceberg. The small part above water can be likened to the conscious mind. The much bigger part beneath the water is like the illimitable depths of your subconscious.

YOUR COMPUTER SYSTEM

As I have said previously, the subconscious mind is like an electronic computer which stores all of the data which are fed to it by the conscious mind. It does not have the ability to reason and it does not have the ability to change this information. Therefore, it is important that you program only correct information and images into your subconscious mind. The only function the subconscious mind can perform, like the electronic computer, is to store and integrate information and if this information is incorrect it will result in incorrect answers unless the material is sent back to the conscious mind for reasoning and logical evaluation.

THE FUNCTION OF THE "CRITICAL FACTOR"

The conscious part of your mind can only think of one thing at a time. Now it is true that the mind may wander and think of a series of different things in rapid succession but at any one instant, it can only be occupied by one thought. Therefore, if we are able to engage the conscious portion of our mind so intently that attention is strongly focused on one idea, we cannot reflect on other things that are happening at that moment. For example, walk up to a person absorbed in watching a tense drama on television and shout, "Stand up!" He will quickly spring to his feet. Only after he has done this will he question your purpose.

The explanation of this phenomenon is really quite simple. He responds to your command because it by-passes the "critical factor" of the conscious mind and goes directly to his subconscious mind. The two prerequisites for this to occur were both present in this situation.

First, his "mental set" (expectation) is correct. Because of the tense drama, almost any sudden noise would have made him jump. Secondly, his conscious mind is so occupied with the drama unfolding that your command registers and is acted upon before it can be examined consciously. You thus completely by-pass his critical factor and your command is accepted without question. Only later does he wonder, "Why did I stand up?"

Thus, an individual is induced into hypnosis by focusing the attention (usually on relaxation) and by-passing the critical factor. This by-pass constitutes the opening wedge into this state. As soon as this occurs, we have established a direct pathway of communication to the subconscious part of the mind. When selective thinking is added in the form of suggestions, hypnosis is achieved. However, when unacceptable suggestions are given to a subject, one of two things will occur. He may either simply reject them or let his critical factor re-enter. In the latter case, the state is destroyed and the subject comes out of hypnosis. I mention this mechanism to allay any fears and misconceptions the reader may still hold.

HETERO-HYPNOSIS AND SELF-HYPNOSIS

In concluding my discussion on medical hypnosis, I will briefly explain the difference between hetero-hypnosis and self-hypnosis. In hetero-hypnosis, someone else acts as the hypnotist and gives you the suggestions. In self-hypnosis, you act as your own hypnotist. At first, it may seem that the suggestions of a hypnotist would be more effective than the suggestions given by yourself. Nevertheless, you must remember that all hypnosis is really self-hypnosis. Whenever the hypnotist gives you a suggestion, you subconsciously rephrase the statement, substituting the pronoun "I" instead of "You." For example, if the hypnotist says to you, "As I count to three, *you* will become very relaxed," you automatically change this suggestion to, "As he counts to three, *I* will become very relaxed."

The best way to learn self-hypnosis is to have a hypnotist give you a post-hypnotic suggestion that a certain procedure agreed upon will allow you to automatically enter hypnosis by yourself.

If you intend to learn self-hypnosis without the services of a hypnotist, you will find the next chapter indispensable. In mastering any new skill, it may take a little longer to learn from a book instead of a personal instructor, but you will take great satisfaction from the fact that you have learned unaided.

I have on record the case histories of numerous patients who felt that they were not able to achieve a deep state of self-hypnosis but who have, nevertheless, conscientiously followed the various techniques I proposed and obtained excellent results from the positive suggestions to their subconscious minds. After all, it is results that count and, while you should strive for a maximum depth, it has been my experience that the most astonishing and satisfactory results can be achieved with very light states of hypnosis. The most important thing is that you learn to by-pass your critical factor and implant selective thoughts. If you can accomplish this, the suggestions will eventually filter into your subconscious mind.

Chapter 8

How to Attain Self-Hypnosis

So Simple A Child Can Do It

DON'T WORRY ABOUT "ROUSING YOURSELF"

A perusal of the literature of hypnosis will show that there are many ways the individual can induce this state in himself. Trial and error should soon indicate the one best suited to your needs, and you will find several helpful guides listed in the bibliography at the end of this book.

Some individuals, having made a decision to learn self-hypnosis in their self-improvement programs, may be concerned, at the start, with the methods used to rouse themselves from this state. They feel, because of many misconceptions, that they might not "come out of it" and remain in a trance indefinitely. This alarm stems from ancient myths and publicity stunts arranged by stage hypnotists. The idea that you might "slumber" on is completely fallacious, yet I feel the untruth is so widespread that a word of reassurance is necessary.

Inasmuch as you know that hypnosis is not sleep, unconsciousness or even a trance in the usual meaning of that word, you should be able to comprehend that rousing yourself is a simple matter which the conscious mind, activating the subconscious mind, can accomplish in a few seconds. One method is to count mentally to three while you are giving yourself suggestions that you will become aroused feeling relaxed and refreshed. As you think of the last number, the cue to terminate hypnosis, your eyes will open and you will be back in your ordinary waking state. An even simpler method is to use the "eye blinking" technique, which will be described subsequently.

Even if you become so relaxed and comfortable that you fall asleep it would make no difference. You would merely nap until your regular "waking up" mechanism aroused you. You would awaken feeling exactly the same way as you would from a nap that had not been preceded by hypnosis.

Briefly, there is no truth to any of the stories you may have heard about persons who could not be roused from the hypnotic state, though I must confess that some individuals resist termination of this state because it is so pleasant. Of course, they are remaining in hypnosis voluntarily, but they come out of it with alacrity once properly motivated to do so. In teaching innumerable patients the techniques of self-hypnosis I have never had any of them experience the slightest difficulty with rousing from the state.

HOW TO ACHIEVE SELF-HYPNOSIS

The method of self-hypnosis that I present in this chapter is the one I have found to be most suited for the reducing regimen I outline in the next chapter. In experimenting with many different techniques I discovered that it is also the one preferred by most patients. The technique is novel in that it is very rapid and so easy that even a child can learn it. As I said earlier, the things that I am going to tell you will be based on personal experience and the experience of many of my successful patients. Space does not permit the description of the standard "eye fixation" method. It requires much more time, and many of my reducing patients were not able to practice it twice daily which is the minimum number of periods required for a reducing program. Because of the time factor, some of my patients gave it up prematurely before they could derive the optimum benefits in their dietary regimen. It became necessary to devise a method which did not require more than a few minutes twice daily. Therefore, in my own medical practice I have come to prefer the simpler and shorter technique described in the following pages.

Nevertheless, I believe that you should be acquainted with the longer and more traditional method since it will give you a better understanding and working knowledge of this most fascinating of nature's states. Melvin Powers, a nationally known Los Angeles hypnotist, gives an excellent description of this classic and time-honored technique, written especially for the layman, in his clear and concise book, *A Practical Guide to Self-Hypnosis,* which is listed in the bibliography. I strongly urge you to get this informative and well-written book.

Although it is to your advantage to have a basic knowledge of other techniques, from a practical standpoint you will find the subsequent directions quite easy to follow. For the sake of clarity, I shall list the seven basic steps.

1. Physical comfort and "mental set."

2. By-passing your critical factor.

3. Obtaining eye-closure.

4. Suggestions for physical relaxation.

5. Compounding the relaxation.

6. Visualization and reducing suggestions,
(including post-hypnotic suggestions).

7. Health suggestions and rousing from the state.

PHYSICAL COMFORT AND "MENTAL SET"

There is no special equipment needed to achieve self-hypnosis. A comfortable chair, a room free from distractions, and the assurance of being undisturbed is all that is needed for the environment. Some individuals prefer a restful sofa or bed so they can fall asleep when self-hypnosis has been completed.

I take it for granted that you have the proper anticipatory attitude (mental set) or you would not be reading this chapter. If you have a negative attitude toward hypnosis, I suggest that you do not begin as you are bound to fail. But if you have a sincere, unreserved desire to experience the pleasant sensation of entering self-hypnosis, all you have to do is follow instructions.

One more remark is necessary about your "expectancy." You should automatically accompany each of the recommended suggestions with these three fundamental attitudes.

1. *"I WANT THIS TO HAPPEN."* (Remember hypnosis is a "consent state.")

2. *"I EXPECT IT TO HAPPEN."* (Generate a belief in your ability to achieve what millions before you have attained. Remember hypnosis is just another one of nature's *normal* states.)

3. *"I WILL WATCH IT HAPPEN."* (Once you begin to respond properly, do not hinder the carrying out of the suggestion by letting your critical factor re-enter and change your mood.)

BY-PASSING YOUR CRITICAL FACTOR

Let us say that you are now comfortable. The exact position you assume is unimportant as long as you are comfortably settled in your chair or bed. As you read the following passage, direct your thoughts along the lines I suggest and actually do the things I ask of you while you are reading the next two paragraphs.

First, I want to teach you to make one of your fingers rigid —so rigid that you will not be able to bend it unless, of course, you change your mind. But for the time being, just for the sake of the experience, *go along with the idea* and do not change your mind. What you will achieve is *NOT HYPNOSIS,* but you will learn to by-pass the critical factor of your conscious mind.

Decide which finger you are going to make rigid while you continue to read. The finger you actually use does not matter, but once you have made your choice, stick to it. Let's suppose you have decided to use your right index finger. Are you ready? Then let's start. Stiffen your index finger. Have you done it? Fine. Let's go on. Now as I count to three in this paragraph, make it more and more stiff with the idea in mind that when I get to *THREE* you will not be able to bend it until you have read to the end of this paragraph. Now, let's start counting. *ONE*...make the finger more rigid...*TWO* ...more rigid yet...make it as rigid as a piece of steel...All right, now you are ready for the last number...*THREE*... make it even stiffer...so stiff and rigid that you just cannot bend it until you finish reading this paragraph...you can try to bend it, but it won't bend at all...that's right, you have made it so completely rigid that it just won't bend...Now, as I count to three once more, it will slowly bend again and feel perfectly normal. *ONE*...bending a little...*TWO*...let it bend some more...and...*THREE*...We have reached the end of this paragraph and the finger is completely flexible and normal—just as it was before you started.

Now you can see how simple and easy that was. *As long as you don't change your mind,* you should have no difficulty in performing this simple procedure. You have merely locked your mind around the idea of a rigid finger, and if you kept this idea foremost in your mind you should have achieved the results you were seeking. Try it once more by reading the previous paragraph over again.

Now, before going on, do it once *without* the book. Count to three yourself this time. The instructions are so simple that there is really nothing to memorize. As I told you, even a child can do it. In my experience it is indeed a rare individual who cannot perform this action. If you happen to be such an individual, then just *PRETEND, IMAGINE,* or *MAKE BELIEVE* that it happens when you go through the motions. That is the important part. Constant repetition will enable you to condition yourself to respond this way automatically. One reason why children are such good hypnotic subjects is that they have excellent imaginations.

Let's briefly analyze exactly what happened. You have kept the thought uppermost in your mind that the finger would not bend until the end of the paragraph. Yet, another part of your mind may have tried to come to the fore by saying, "Oh, this is ridiculous. Of course, I can bend my finger." Immediately, the most concentrated part of your mind then said, "No, be quiet; I can't bend it at all—see— I am trying and it won't bend." In other words, you have by-passed the critical part of your mind by ignoring it and accepting instead an illogical suggestion as fact. That is what I mean by locking your mind around an idea.

Even though the above procedure can be performed in less than a minute, I have spent much time in explaining the intricacies of this phenomenon. It is important because by-passing the critical factor is the entering wedge into hypnosis. To achieve the hypnotic state, you then simply implant selective thinking in the form of suggestions. Once you have grasped this fundamental principle the rest is even easier.

I cannot believe that any of my readers are still having difficulty with this procedure. But for that unusual individual, one more word of explanation is in order. Even though that finger was not as rigid as you would have liked it to be, you, too, will be able to do this as long as you keep practicing it.

This is similar to two swimmers about to enter the cold water of a pool. One will jump in quickly, the other will go into the water slowly—step by step. Ultimately, both swimmers will completely submerge in the water.

The person who is afraid to lock his mind completely around an idea and leaves himself a little opening, is like the second swimmer. Eventually, he, too, will succeed, but since this feeling of the "lock" is a new experience to him, he takes it slowly, in steps. With repeated experience, he conditions himself to respond completely. He realizes that his initial reluctance was due to a false sense of "losing control" when actually he was learning to gain more control over his body.

OBTAINING EYE-CLOSURE

You are now ready for the next step. I am going to ask you to repeat the rigid finger maneuver once more with one slight change in procedure. After your finger is stiff, suggest to yourself, "As my finger bends, my eyes will close so that by the end of my third count my eyes will be shut and my eyelids will be so relaxed and limp that they will not work or open *UNLESS I LET THE TENSION COME BACK*

INTO THEM BY BLINKING. I want this to happen, I expect it to happen, and I will watch it happen." The words are not important but be sure you grasp the idea.

As soon as your finger is rigid, open your eyes *wide* and *DO NOT BLINK THEM* from then on because you are going to condition yourself to rouse yourself from the hypnotic state by blinking your eyelids. Since you now wish to enter into the state, let them close slowly without blinking. After they are closed, keep your mind focused on every little sensation that you feel in your eye muscles and let them develop a progressive feeling of relaxation until they seem so relaxed that it is just too much effort to make them work or open. At this point you may again use your imagination just as you did with the finger, the only difference being that now you pursue relaxation rather than rigidity. When you have locked your mind around the idea that your eyes are so relaxed they will not work or open, test them to make sure they will not open unless, of course, you blink them. You now have "eye-closure."

Next, blink your eyes and feel them pop open!

Some individuals notice a "fluttering sensation" in their eyelids upon achieving eye closure. This is a perfectly normal reaction and indicates an excellent state of relaxation of the eyelid muscles.

I suggest you read the last several paragraphs over again and try it a few times before reading on. Notice how little time it takes to go through the whole procedure. Do you believe me now when I say that there is nothing difficult to this procedure as long as you know what to do? Now, let's go on.

SUGGESTIONS FOR PHYSICAL RELAXATION

After having obtained complete relaxation of the eye muscles through eye-closure, you next wish to send this relaxed feeling all the way down to your toes. You should let yourself feel this relaxation go all the way down the body to your feet. This should be very easy to do.

If you prefer mental pictures, you might imagine yourself like a rag doll, with arms and legs limp and dangling down as you send the relaxation throughout your body. Use whatever visualization you find most effective. Imagine that if someone were to pick up your arm and drop it, it would just flop down like a wet dish cloth.

COMPOUNDING THE RELAXATION

Once you have obtained eye-closure and feel nicely relaxed from head to toe, you are entering into a state of hypnosis. At this point you could start your reducing suggestions. Nevertheless, when you are first learning to enter this state you should also employ the following simple deepening procedure. It adds less than one minute to the induction time.

Give yourself a suggestion such as this: "In a moment, I am going to blink my eyes and they will open. I will then close them again, and as I close them the next time I will find myself three times more deeply relaxed than I am right now."

Proceed to do as planned. As you close your eyes you will feel a very pleasant surge of relaxation which you allow to travel down to your toes. This was your first repetition of eye-closure—your first compounding of the suggestion.

Now, compound it once more, while thinking these thoughts:

"I will open my eyes once more by blinking them. But when I close them the next time, I will be twice as relaxed as I am now. I will feel so completely relaxed that every last bit of tension in my body will have disappeared—I will just let myself be covered by a blanket of relaxation from head to toe."

Again, proceed as planned. You have now completed your second compounding. Notice how, as each new suggestion is added, the previous ones seem to become more effective. Actually, the whole basic principle of hypnosis is based on this premise of compounding suggestions. As one belief is added to another, you become more convinced of your ability to achieve a deeper state of relaxation.

If you have followed instructions thus far, you should feel quite pleased at the almost unbelievable state of deep relaxation you have achieved. Remember, as you repeat this procedure daily you will be able to achieve even deeper states each time. The reason for this should be quite obvious to you since you must realize by now the role conditioning plays in this process.

THE FRYING PAN TECHNIQUE

This procedure is not ordinarily a routine part of your induction, but I include it here to illustrate how you may use mental pictures to deepen whatever relaxation you may have already achieved. I use the following example because my patients have told me that it seems to be one of the most effective visualizations they have utilized. In fact, a number of them use it to help them relax in preparation for going to sleep, often obviating the need for tranquilizers. Here is the technique:

After you have induced self-hypnosis, mentally picture a piece of butter in a frying pan. Visualize the pan sitting on top of a burner and beginning to warm up. Now imagine that you are melting like the pat of butter and make suggestions to yourself as follows:

"In a moment I am going to take a deep breath. When I

let it out, I will feel my body sink further into this chair (or bed) just as if I were melting like this piece of butter."

Now take a deep breath and hold it as long as you can with comfort. While your lungs are full, clearly visualize the butter beginning to melt in the pan. Then let all the air out, as you imagine your entire body actually "melting." Some of my patients report a pleasant, warm flush goes through them as they perform this procedure. If you experience such a sensation you may let this relax you even more. Breathe slowly and evenly, letting yourself become more warm and limp with each breath.

VISUALIZATIONS AND REDUCING SUGGESTIONS

Let me briefly review the whole procedure thus far. You start by getting into a comfortable position, by-pass the critical factor by using the rigid finger technique, followed by eye-closure. Next you send the relaxation throughout your entire body and compound it twice by the eye-opening-and-closing method. It takes my average patient about three minutes to complete these steps. After several weeks of practice, most of them have automatically begun to develop a short cut.

Here is what they do. They close their eyes relaxing and then testing them to make sure they will not work or open. Attaining immediate eye-closure, they then send the feeling of relaxation down to the feet and start with the visualizations and post-hypnotic suggestions for reducing described in the next chapter. They are ready to rouse themselves and return to the ordinary waking state or are ready to fall asleep if it is bedtime, all within a period of five minutes.

You must admit there are very few individuals who cannot spare five minutes twice daily for such an important health problem as obesity. Furthermore, remember that the benefit you obtain from five minutes of relaxation while in hypnosis is equivalent to a much longer period of plain non-scientific relaxation.

HEALTH SUGGESTIONS AND ROUSING FROM THE STATE

Once you have decided that you are ready to return to the ordinary waking state, you should always give yourself health suggestions. One way is as follows:

"In a moment, I am going to rouse myself from my present state. I will feel refreshed, alert, and completely comfortable. All the post-hypnotic suggestions that I have given to myself will assist me in reaching my goals and I will feel better than I have in a long time. Each time I enter self-hypnosis I will achieve the state more rapidly and deeply."

Now blink your eyes (the signal for rousing) and just as you are opening them, think to yourself, "I *do* feel fine." Remember, you are still in a hypersuggestible state at this point of transition and you might as well take advantage of it by implanting one last healthful idea.

SIMPLICITY IS THE KEY WORD

There you have it in a nutshell. This whole technique may sound too simple to you and you might think, "How can something as easy as this really work?"

Actually, there is really nothing complicated about self-hypnosis as soon as you discard your former misconceptions. By now you probably realize that the state of hypnosis is something entirely different than what you had imagined. You certainly didn't feel "unconscious" but you felt extremely relaxed and actually superaware of whatever you focused your attention on. The reason, of course, is that you had cleared your mind of all the usual distractions present in the ordinary waking state.

There may still be a few individuals among my readers who feel that they have not achieved hypnosis. This is a common attitude among beginners. Since you really do not know what you are looking for in this new experience, it may be difficult for you to accept the idea that you were truly hypnotized. Nevertheless, I urge you to continue to act as though you were in this state, and continue with the reducing suggestions outlined in the next chapter. Not only will you set up a conditioned reflex pattern permitting you to achieve a deeper state each time, but as you notice the results in your reducing program you will not be able to deny that something has happened which has benefited you a great deal in your battle of the bulge. In the final analysis it is the results that count.

TESTING FOR THE STATE

In closing this chapter I wish to mention one more facet of self-hypnosis which I have left till last because it is not part of your regular technique. For those hypercritical and doubting individuals who are too impatient to await the beneficial results in their reducing program and who must be convinced that they are in hypnosis before such results can become evident, I will mention several tests they may perform to prove to themselves that they are in a hypersuggestible state.

After you have achieved eye-closure and physical relaxation, you might suggest to yourself that on the count of three you will notice the development of tingling in a hand. Then slowly count to three as you focus your attention on every little sensation in that portion of your body, using a mental picture to reinforce the suggestion. Once you have achieved the desired results, always remove the suggestion.

Melvin Powers, in the book I mentioned earlier in this chapter, describes 15 different tests you may perform. I again recommend that you consult this volume for supplementary reading. For the sake of completeness, I will describe in detail one of my favorite tests to illustrate how they work.

THE SALIVA TEST

This test will demonstrate to you that your imagination is a much more powerful medium of self-control than will power. First enter self-hypnosis, then picture someone in your mind's eye whose likeness you can readily visualize. Let us say, for instance, your physician. First, see your physician standing in front of you (with your eyes closed, of course). When you have a good image of him, look at the details of the picture. See the white coat he may be wearing, the color of the tie he has on, the color of his hair, the color and texture of his trousers, and even the color and shape of his shoes. Once you have a sharp and detailed picture, look at his hands and observe him holding a lemon in his left palm. Wait until you see it clearly. Then visualize him taking a knife and cutting the lemon in half. As he cuts the lemon in half, watch him taking one half of the lemon with his right hand, leaving the other half in his left hand.

Now observe his *right* hand. Notice him *squeeze* the lemon and witness the juice running down and filling a glass. As this occurs, you will become aware of an increased flow of saliva in your mouth.

Next focus your attention on his *left* hand as he takes the other half of the lemon to his mouth and draws on it. At this point, you may even fantasy the sucking noise that he makes with his mouth. Now notice him swallow the acrid lemon juice. Imagine the sour taste. As you scrutinize this scene, you will notice a steady increase in the flow of saliva in your mouth. Now contemplate the following thoughts: "As I continue to watch my doctor sucking on this lemon and the flow of saliva increases in my mouth, I will count to three, and when I get to three, I will have an uncontrollable urge to swallow— I *want* this to happen; I *expect* it to happen; I will *watch* it happen." Now slowly count to three and when you get to three, give way to your compulsion to swallow.

I have had a number of patients tell me that they could even "smell" or "taste" the lemon in visualizing the scene.

In closing this discussion, I wish to remind the reader once more that he does not have to wait until he becomes an expert to start with specific reducing suggestions. Once you have learned the finger test and eye-closure and send the relaxation throughout your body, you can start with therapeutic suggestions and visual imagery.

I have included various refinements and some additional steps mainly for the purpose of giving you a better understanding of the principles of the self-hypnotic technique. Of the procedures presented, you will eventually find one that will become your favorite.

Now let's get to work on the core of this book and start studying Chapter Nine.

Chapter 9

Your Subconscious Mind Will Help

Put Your Imagination to Work

PUTTING THEORY TO WORK

This is the chapter that will teach you how to utilize the theories explained earlier in the book. Everything that has been written thus far has been leading up to the application of self-hypnosis to your weight problem. Therefore, most of the discussion will concern the techniques you will have to learn if you wish to lose weight and maintain that loss. By this time you should be familiar with the basic theories upon which these techniques are based. Now you must put them to work for you.

You have already taken your first practical step toward solving your obesity problem by beginning to practice the verbal and visual formula that results in self-hypnosis. The very fact that you have made a beginning should give you a feeling of great satisfaction. You are already on the way to solving a problem that has made your life less enjoyable than it will be when you have reduced to your correct weight.

MENTAL PICTURES

Seeing yourself as you wish to be in your mind's eye is the basis for success in every endeavor. You would find it difficult to find a baseball rookie who has not imagined himself leading the league in home runs. The actor playing a bit part has been "seeing" himself as a star for years. And the junior executive, although I have no way of proving this, imagines himself seated at a desk with a dozen phones claiming his constant attention.

Be that as it may, you *must* come to believe that the proper and constant use of mental pictures will eventually destroy your old self-image and replace it with one that embraces everything you desire. The history of successful people proves that if you dream about your goal long enough your chances of achieving it are increased a thousand-fold. Of course, dreams or mental pictures must be reinforced by actual practice in your daily activities. You cannot dream off weight any more than you can dream yourself into the president's chair at General Motors.

The total concept of the self-image is discussed at length by Dr. Maxwell Maltz in *Psycho-Cybernetics* which is listed in the bibliography, and I suggest you get it if you wish to learn all about this fascinating subject.

For your purpose—the losing of weight and maintaining that loss—it is essential that you have a clear mental picture of how you wish to look. You must keep this picture uppermost in your mind from the time you start employing self-hypnosis to aid you in dieting until your motivation for reducing is so strongly imbedded in your subconscious that responses are automatic.

HELPFUL HINTS

If, at some time in your past life, you have been slim or at the correct weight for your body structure, find a photograph of yourself taken at that time and make it your physical ideal.

Those of you who have been overweight as long as you can remember can always find a picture of some person who is approximately your height, has your general body structure and resembles you somewhat in facial features. Make this person who, of course, should not be overweight, your ideal. Let his or her picture become your "new image."

Another helpful device, one that my patients have used with great success, is to purchase an attractive dress or suit that is several sizes too small for you. It need not be expensive. The main requirement is that it must be small enough so that you can wear it only after you have reduced to your correct weight. This provides strong motivation and it will increase even more if you hang it in a prominent place in your closet where you can admire it daily and try it on from time to time, finding that either the garment is getting bigger or you are getting smaller. The latter is the better assumption.

Each day, before going into self-hypnosis, take a long look at the photograph of your former self or the picture you have chosen. Next, enter hypnosis and while in the state visualize yourself wearing the attractive garment you have purchased.

Incidentally, the money you spend on this garment will not be wasted. You *will* be able to wear it some day although the ladies particularly may have to make alterations as a concession to changing styles. Perhaps we should say your goal should be to lose weight fast enough (but consistent with safety) so that you can wear the garment before it goes out of style.

When you have reached a satisfactory depth of hypnosis, examine your new image in detail. Notice how well you look with that stomach flat and only one chin. Notice the trim appearance you present with your hips slimmed down.

Look at the graceful silhouette you have with your posterior reduced to normal proportions. Before terminating the hypnotic state, give yourself the suggestion that each succeeding time you hypnotize yourself you will go into a deeper state and that your new image will become more clear, life-like and *attainable*.

THE SUBCONSCIOUS FEEL

It is important that you produce a feeling of elation as you contemplate your new image. The more you program this mental picture into your subconscious mind, the more you will notice you are gaining a feeling of confidence in your ability to achieve your goal. It is this "subconscious feel" that indicates your subconscious mind is beginning to accept a new memory pattern and is actually storing a picture of you that is your ideal. Of course, the picture is really not in accord with the truth at the present time, but the subconscious, as has been stated, cannot reason and it accepts your evaluation as correct. The result is that the conscious mind aquires a feeling of self-esteem that is so important to the continuance of your diet program.

In the beginning, it is likely you will be able to attain this high regard for yourself only while you are in the hypnotic state but gradually the feeling will spill over into your normal waking moments. Because of this reciprocal interaction between the two minds, you will actually begin to feel and act like a new person long before the results you seek are accomplished. This affords a tremendous incentive to maintain your dietary program.

The best way I can describe this feeling to you before you experience it for yourself is to use an example that will be familiar to you if you have ever taken part in a stage play. If you have portrayed a certain character in a play long enough there will be times when you feel you *are* the person you represent. While you are in front of the audience you actually "lose" your own identity although, at the same time, your underlying sense of reality assures you that you are "just pretending." When you do this you temporarily alter your self-image in order to better portray the character intended by the writer and director. You learn, as actors say, to "live the part."

This ability to change the self-image explains why some famous comedians are quite serious in their private lives.

A DREAM BECOMES A REALITY

If you imagine something long enough and hard enough, it will tend to become a reality. We are all familiar with the actor who eventually comes to believe his own exaggerated publicity.

During the war, there were many service men who pretended to have severe backaches in order to get away from the battlefield. The peculiar result was that some of these soldiers pretended so long that ultimately they actually developed such backaches. They had declared they had backaches so often that their subconscious minds eventually accepted it as a fact. Response to treatment was poor.

In the same vein, I remember a young housewife, who used to feign a headache whenever she was confronted with a social situation which created anxiety. This gave her an excuse not to face the problem. However, after a number of years of "make believe" headaches, she finally began to have real headaches whenever she was confronted by a similar intolerable situation. When she consulted me for treatment, she was seeking relief from these headaches because they were interfering with her social life.

In much the same way, as you contemplate your new image, your personality begins to take on the characteristics of one who is confident he can surmount all obstacles. It takes on this new aspect because you have already begun to learn the part you have chosen to portray. Do not doubt that this subtle transformation will take place. My overweight patients invariably begin to think and act thin long before they reach their goal.

FROM STILL PICTURES TO MOTION PICTURES

Once you have become adept at seeing yourself as you wish to be, the next step is to see yourself acting as this slim "you" would act in various situations. For instance, the next time you are in self-hypnosis, see your new image at a pleasant gathering being congratulated by your friends on your attractive appearance. See yourself dancing gracefully and displaying great energy which makes you the envy of your friends sitting on the sidelines.

The situations may be varied to suit your taste. For example, you can see yourself at the beach in an attractive bathing suit with a swarm of the opposite sex paying you a great deal of attention. The main thing is to visualize yourself doing things you now forego and receiving recognition because you no longer have a lumpy unattractive figure.

Many working girls I have treated, like to visualize themselves as the "queen bee" in the office with hordes of handsome men gathered around their desks. It is doubtful if they could get much work done in this situation but the picture pleases them. Such a mental picture can be a strong motivating force in dieting.

VISUAL IMAGERY PROVIDES A BONUS

I am sure all of you have known the woman who has just lost weight and complains that her hips are too big, her lower abdomen still bulges, and her thighs are too fat. She states that she does not like to lose weight because she always loses in the "wrong places." This occurs even when proper excercise is performed along with the reducing program.

I would like to tell you now of some curious and still inexplicable results I have encountered in patients who have combined visual imagery with self-hypnosis. For a number of years I have made it a practice to photograph patients before they begin their diets and take another picture when they have reached their ideal weight. In comparing the "after" photographs of patients who reduced by combining visual imagery with self-hypnosis, I have reached the inescapable conclusion that their figures are better proportioned than the figures of those who reduced without the aid of mental pictures.

My findings have been further reinforced by the fact that patients who have reduced more than once—the first time without the use of mental pictures and the second time with visual imagery added—show such a degree of difference that it would be difficult to deny that the additional and constant use of mental pictures favorably influences body proportions.

There is no provable scientific reason to explain this unusual result as yet but psychosomatic medicine sheds some light on the way it may happen.

Psychosomatic medicine, although it has masqueraded under a multiplicity of labels for centuries, is a comparatively new branch of the healing arts in its present form. One of the theories it has proved is that the mind can produce symptoms of organic disease although tests show that no organic disease is present.

We already know that the mind can affect the functioning of our glands. An excellent example of this phenomenon is found in the woman who, after being sterile for years, suddenly believes that she is pregnant despite the fact that tests indicate that she is not. Menstruation ceases, morning sickness ensues, the abdomen and breasts enlarge, and she manifests all the clinical symptoms of pregnancy. Some of these women carry their "baby" to term and finally admit they were not pregnant only after prolonged labor contractions produce nothing more than a discharge resembling the menstrual flow. Physicians call this condition pseudocyesis and it is not as rare as you may believe.

It is a well known fact that an emotionally caused delayed menstrual period can often be started by hypnotic suggestion. If the mind can have such a powerful influence on the sex glands, it is certainly conceivable that it may also have a similar effect on the pituitary and other glands of the body which are responsible for its fat distribution.

Please do not misinterpret this commentary. As I have stated, there is no substantial proof of how this happens. I simply mention it as an interesting finding. I would be most delighted to hear from any of my readers about similar experiences.

YOUR "NEW IMAGE" AND FOOD

Remember, up to now, your subconscious mind has had memory patterns of frustration in handling various exposures to fattening foods. That is why, on a conscious level, you may have thought, "What's the use of going on a diet? I'll only gain it all back again!" You have the memory of failure implanted in your subconscious mind. Therefore, you must substitute a picture of success.

Most of you have had dreams so vivid that their effect stayed with you for days or even months and years. Although self-hypnosis differs from sleep, impressions are just as vivid and are stored in the subconscious mind as permanent memories. You can readily see the advantage of this in keeping your new self-image in the forefront of your thoughts.

For example, suppose that every Sunday evening you are invited to a friend's home or you are in the habit of eating out in a restaurant. In the past, you may have dieted through will power all week long, but when Sunday arrives you order everything on the menu—or, if in the friend's home, you take second and third helpings. You have been behaving this way for so long that you may not even give it any thought and do it unconsciously.

The idea is to change this habit pattern. The method is as follows: While in the state of self-hypnosis, visualize your new image wearing a fashionable garment at this particular dinner. See yourself taking small portions of food, eating slower, enjoying the taste of foods more, and slowly savoring every bite. In other words, "get more mileage" out of the foods you eat. When it is time for second helpings and dessert, you instinctively refuse because you have already gratified your taste buds to their utmost. It is very important that you visualize all this in detail. If you have achieved a deep state, you might even be able to fantasy the aroma of the food, just as some of the patients could actually "smell" the lemon in the saliva test. The more different senses you can bring into play, the more realistic and beneficial it will be.

If you happen to be one of those persons who have been trained to "clean the plate" (and most obese people have), then imagine yourself being so delighted and gratified by the taste of the food, you always leave a small amount of food on your platter. As you glance at the food remaining on your plate, it indicates to you that you will weigh that much less the next day.

After you have repeatedly programmed this type of visual

imagery into your subconscious mind, eventually, when you are actually exposed to this situation on Sunday night, you will almost instinctively behave the way you saw yourself act in the visualization.

THE POWER OF VISUAL IMAGERY

In case you still have some doubt regarding the effectiveness of such a technique, I would like to describe an experiment conducted by a team of investigators who reported the results in *Research Quarterly*.

To illustrate the effect of visual imagery, a team of basketball players was divided into three groups. One group practiced shooting baskets 20 minutes every day for two weeks. The second group, the neutral or control group necessary for research, did nothing. The third group simply visualized themselves successfully shooting baskets for 20 minutes daily.

The results were astonishing. An improvement of 24 percent was shown by the first group. The second group, as might be supposed, showed no improvement. But the third group, none of whose members had touched a basketball, improved 23 percent. This is as strong a recommendation of visual imagery as it is possible to find although many other tests have had similar results. This has also been proved by a New York golf instructor who guarantees to take 10 strokes off of anybody's game if they will just visualize themselves playing perfectly and stay away from the golf course for a week.

I do not mean to imply that you could learn any skill, like playing the piano, simply by imagining yourself doing so without any actual practice. However, if you were to compare practicing with and without the mental pictures, the results using the imagery would be far beyond your usual expectations.

Similarly you will achieve better results in reducing if you use mental pictures to substitute correct habit patterns for your previous faulty ones.

USING POST-HYPNOTIC SUGGESTIONS

A post-hypnotic suggestion is a suggestion you give to yourself while in hypnosis. It becomes effective upon giving yourself a specific signal after you have returned to the ordinary waking state. This principle of medical hypnosis can be used to your advantage when confronted by a tempting food situation.

Once you have learned to produce the subconscious feel (that feeling of confidence in your ability to achieve your goal) whenever you visualize your new image while in self-hypnosis, you are ready to give yourself a post-hypnotic suggestion to reproduce this "feel." First you must decide upon the signal that you will use. One of the most effective signals for my patients has been a wallet-sized picture of the physical ideal previously described. Some patients have found a small card with the word "*SLENDER*" written on it just as effective. This can easily be carried in your wallet or purse.

While in the state of self-hypnosis, produce the image and the feel and give yourself the following suggestion. "From now on, whenever I wish to reproduce this feeling of enjoying my new attractive figure and the confidence in my ability to attain this goal, I will look at the photograph of my physical ideal."

Give yourself this post-hypnotic suggestion every time you practice self-hypnosis. Test the signal as often as is convenient during your ordinary waking activities. Repeat this process until, by means of conditioning, the response to the signal is as strong as you would like it to be.

Now you are ready to utilize this technique each time you are exposed to a food which has a tendency to make you deviate from your diet, or when you feel yourself slipping in maintaining your proper positive mental attitude. You will find this much more effective than will power.

Consider the following example to illustrate this method. If you happen to be bored with the monotony of your work, with no particular craving for food, but in the mood to "raid the ice box" just for "something to do," use your signal. Look at the photograph and activate the subconscious feel. The amount of pleasure you derive from the mental picture of your new image added to the feeling of confidence in your ability to achieve your goal will make it much easier for you to overcome this temptation. The amount of pleasure you might derive from the temporary gratification of your taste buds will, indeed, seem small in comparison.

You might wonder how such a signal technique can work and activate a feeling. I can best explain this by giving an analogy from everyday experience.

Have you ever heard a song and have it bring back memories of a pleasant experience? As this occurs, you have a temporary *feeling of nostalgia.*

Similarly, if you have ever been in another country, you might remember having seen something which suddenly made you *feel homesick.*

In other words, the song, or the thing you saw in the foreign country (like the signal) reproduced in you a *feeling that you had experienced before.* The reason, of course, is that this feeling had become a conditioned response by repeated association.

A METHOD OF VERBAL SUGGESTIONS

The basic principle of this program rests upon the use of imagery. Nevertheless, occasionally you may wish to use verbal suggestions in addition. However, I wish to point out that there are two essential rules to be observed in applying verbal suggestions to the reducing regimen. From personal experience with many patients, I have arrived at the following general conclusions.

1. Use only *positive* suggestions.

2. Have a clear idea of what the suggestion should be *prior* to entering self-hypnosis.

A suggestion such as "food will taste bad to me and I will not overeat" is called a negative suggestion and is usually either very short-lived or completely ineffective. The same idea can be expressed in a positive manner as follows. "Foods allowed on my diet will taste so good to me and be so satisfying that I will require less of them and have very little need to eat between meals."

An attempt to figure out how to word a suggestion while in self-hypnosis may require too much conscious effort and thus interfere with the relaxation obtained. Therefore, my patients have found the following simple method very effective.

First, decide what you wish to accomplish. Then write the suggestion on a piece of paper, expressing the main idea. Next, slowly read the words over to yourself three times. Now induce self-hypnosis and for about 30 to 60 seconds just remain passive and let the words come back to you without giving yourself any further conscious suggestions. Many patients report that the words will seem to come back in a spontaneous, almost automatic manner. Whatever happens, do not make any conscious effort to remember what was on the paper. As long as you have by-passed your critical factor, your subconscious mind will begin to accept the basic idea.

In my experience, short periods (up to one minute) of verbal suggestions implanted daily are much more effective than using longer periods at less frequent intervals.

An example of a good "mental set" suggestion should be worded somewhat like this:

"I TRULY BELIEVE THAT I AM CAPABLE OF DIETING SUCCESSFULLY AND EFFORTLESSLY, TO ACHIEVE AND MAINTAIN MY GOAL OF A HEALTHY AND ATTRACTIVE BODY. IN THIS, I AM GUIDED BY MY CONFIDENCE IN THE NATURAL POWERS WITHIN ME."

Patients tell me that another very effective suggestion is as follows:

"WHENEVER I AM TEMPTED TO EAT FATTENING FOOD, I WILL AUTOMATICALLY ASK MYSELF, 'DO I REALLY WANT TO INDULGE MYSELF? WON'T I FEEL BETTER IF I EXERCISE THE SELF-CONTROL TECHNIQUE I HAVE LEARNED?'"

Using the above two examples as models, you can make up your own suggestions.

DISCOVER YOUR "BELLS"

Earlier in the book I went to some length in showing you how bell-food responses occur. When you finish this chapter it would be helpful to you if you listed all the bells or, more properly, situations to which you react by eating. You should sit down with paper and pencil and enumerate every situation that is causing you to eat at the present time. Excluding your appetite at mealtime, you may find you have learned to respond to dozens of circumstances by nibbling between meals or overeating at regular meal times. Most of my patients have been astounded when they finally completed listing all the "cues" that resulted in eating.

I will list for you some of the most common situations as reported by my patients. Among them you may find some that apply to your obesity problem.

(1) JUST RELAXING.

    (a) Being up at night after others are asleep.

    (b) Watching television.

    (c) Entertaining company in my home.

    (d) Upon first getting home from work or school.

(2) DURING ROUTINE ACTIVITIES.

    (a) While writing letters, reading, studying, or sewing.

    (b) Doing housework, or driving my car with food in the seat next to me.

(3) WHEN VERY BUSY.

    (a) Crowded for time and "too busy" to prepare proper meals for myself.

    (b) Grabbing a quick snack for a "pick up."

(4) WHEN AWAY FROM HOME.

    (a) Visiting in the homes of friends or relatives.

    (b) Eating in restaurants.

    (c) Urged by friends to try their "special recipes."

    (d) Attending receptions and parties.

(5) BEING CONFRONTED BY
FOOD SITUATIONS.

    (a) Cooking or preparing foods.

    (b) Getting home first from the market and putting foods away.

(c) Cleaning table at end of meal and putting left-overs away.

(d) Opening refrigerator door.

(e) Seeing other people eating fattening foods, especially if I have already finished eating.

(f) Seeing and smelling delicious but fattening foods even though I am already full.

(g) Compulsion to buy wrong foods when shopping in well-stocked supermarket.

(6) MOODS OF DEPRESSION AND DESPAIR.

(a) Having just weighed myself and finding that I haven't lost after a "starvation diet."

(b) Just plain bored and alone with "nothing to do."

(c) Worrying about other members of my family.

(d) When any kind of crisis occurs.

(e) Rewarding myself after a trying day.

I have categorized these bell situations for the sake of simplicity. However, you should make up your own individualized list recording each specific situation on a separate line.

Your next step is to decide exactly what you can do to handle each situation. You will be able to avoid some of them, but most of them will have to be resolved and rendered harmless. To say, "I simply shouldn't do that" is of no value. You must find something more constructive and of a positive nature that you can do instead of eating the improper foods. Your physician will be able to help you by outlining the steps necessary to handle those circumstances which give you the most difficulty. Be sure to take advantage of his sage advice based on his professional training and years of experience.

Again, I urge you to record on paper how you plan to overcome each problem. In carrying out your course of action, self-hypnosis will be of inestimable value. This may either be done by verbal suggestion or preferably by mental pictures in which you see yourself circumventing or rising above the situations, according to your preconceived plan. You will not be able to resolve all these situations at once but constant repetition of visualizations in which you behave successfully will eventually result in a conditioned response which will obviate your constant recalling them all to mind every day. Negative feedback will keep you on the right track.

AN EXAMPLE OF CHANGING YOUR CONDITIONED RESPONSE

Suppose that one of your predicaments arises from your weekly visit to a certain friend's home where coffee is always served together with cookies that are forbidden on your diet. Your hostess invariably urges you to take just one of the delicacies which she claims to have made "especially for you."

You have decided to solve this problem by courteously refusing these sweets while commenting on the excellence of her coffee. You plan to sip slowly several cups of coffee until all the cookies have been devoured by the other guests.

You then incorporate the mental pictures of your corrected behavior in your daily hypnotic sessions. Make the visualization as detailed as possible, leaving nothing to chance. You might even go so far as to imagine the exact words you will speak in response to your insistent hostess' remark, "Just tasting *one* won't hurt you!"

You should observe your new, slim self-image answering firmly and confidently, "I appreciate your good intentions, but since my doctor does not allow me to eat cookies, I would feel quite depressed after my next weight check at his office. I would have to admit failure in carrying out his orders. Besides, I'm sure you wouldn't really want me to do something that's bad for my health." After programming this memory pattern into your subconscious mind for a reasonable period of time, you will be quite pleased at the facility with which you will be able to carry out the correct response, rather than letting yourself be led astray by this formerly disturbing situation.

MEASURING YOUR SUCCESS

As you are progressing with these methods, you will want to evaluate your success. The amount of weight you have lost is obviously the most simple method. Nevertheless, it has one important drawback. After an initial comparatively rapid loss of weight, most of which usually represents loss of water, your body exerts a stabilizing effect upon further reduction in total body weight. Even though you have adhered to your diet, there may be a period of several weeks when the scale shows no change.

This is a most crucial point in your reducing program because you may become discouraged and feel as one of my patients so adequately expressed it when she said, "I feel like I am hitting my head against a brick wall." As I have repeatedly stated in this book, such a negative attitude is at the very basis of most failures while reducing. You are apt to rationalize, saying "What's the use," and deviate from your diet. Therefore, it is of utmost importance that you prevent the occurrence of this negative change in your attitude.

First you must realize that this is a perfectly normal phenomenon. Unfortunately, we do not have a scale that weighs only body fat, but one that weighs only your total weight which includes the measurement of tissue fluids, bowel and bladder contents. Even though there may be a steady decline in your adipose deposits, the composite body weight may fluctuate in response to variations in these other factors.

Noting your change in total weight from one month to the next will serve as an accurate gauge of how well you are slimming down the fat. Yet, to assist your weekly progress, another yardstick is needed, namely, "HOW WELL HAVE I ADHERED TO MY DIET?" This criterion will naturally parallel your long-term weight loss, but does not always agree with it on a weekly basis for the reasons given.

It should be obvious to you that if you are not achieving the expected results, there are only two possible causes. Either you have not stuck to your diet, or the diet is not strict enough. In the latter instance, your physician can make the proper changes, but unless both factors are known, you cannot possibly have a true picture of your weekly progress. Therefore, in order to prevent a despairing attitude because of a seemingly hopeless situation, you must keep an accurate record of your actual dietary performance. Only such a record will give you a true picture of how successful your use of self-hypnosis has been.

KEEPING A FOOD DIARY

The adoption of the following step is an absolutely essential part of your reducing program. Experience has taught me that its omission may often lead to eventual failure. In order to correct your mistakes with the aid of self-hypnosis, you must first know what they are, and there is no better way than a weekly review of your recorded food diary. Remember that *diet is a treatment and not a cure* for obesity. To attain the latter you must achieve permanent correction of your mistakes, that is, your faulty eating habits.

If you do not wish to carry a notebook, a single 8½″ by 11″ sheet of paper has been found to be quite adequate by my patients. When folded, it is easily slipped into your pocket or purse. In the appendix at the end of this book, you will find a suggested form which is easily made up.

You must carry this paper with you at all times and write down every bit of food or drink you consume during the day and night, since you are prone to "forget" some of the little snacks you eat. You must make a notation every time any food or drink is ingested. Jotting them down at the end of each day is not an accurate way to keep track of your total caloric intake.

It is important that you be truthful, because at the end of each seven days you should review your past week's diary and compare it to your prescribed diet. Next, circle in red pencil all the mistakes you have made. If the total number of errors decreases from week to week, it indicates that you are making satisfactory progress regardless of what the scale shows. I have yet to find an instance when self-hypnosis has not shown a definitely beneficial effect as long as the principles outlined in this book were followed.

PROFIT FROM YOUR ERRORS

Above everything else, do not let initial failures prevent you from continuing your dietary regimen. You have been many years accumulating your faulty eating habits and they cannot be eliminated in a day, a week or even a month. Give yourself at least six months to try the methods outlined in this book. If you do you will show results so apparent, both physiologically and psychologically, that you will never want to return to your slipshod methods of eating and the excuses you have devised to rationalize that eating or, to be more exact, overeating.

It is almost certain that you will "fall off your diet" in the initial stages of your reducing program. This is to be expected until the conditioned reflex has been established but you must avoid one common pitfall. DO NOT TRY TO JUSTIFY YOUR MISTAKES, BUT ADMIT YOUR ERRORS. Try to think of your first failures as stepping stones to success rather than permanent road blocks. It is the latter feeling that causes many persons to give up dieting before they have gotten fairly started. "Yes, Doctor, I know I went off my diet, BUT—" is the usual way these excuses and rationalizations begin. Then—"It was my birthday," —or—"I had worked hard all day so I thought one little piece wouldn't hurt." (Notice the reward theme.) Be honest with yourself from the start. Defending your faults simply cultivates the seeds of failure.

BUT is a word you simply cannot afford to use in dieting. It is far better to take the following steps.

1. Admit your error.
2. Analyze why and how it happened.
3. Develop a method of correcting it.
4. Utilize self-hypnosis to help you in carrying out the correction.
5. Measure your success in following the first four steps by noting your response in similar and subsequent situations.

Do you recognize the feedback process? You merely handle your mistakes as bells that you must heed to change your faulty conditioned response.

AN EXAMPLE OF THE FEEDBACK TECHNIQUE

Suppose, as you review your slip-ups each week, you find that occasionally you still nibble on candy or chocolate while

111

watching television. Ordinarily, you would protest—"*BUT* —I just can't help myself when I see those luscious food commercials." Be that as it may, you decide to overcome this hurdle. Therefore, you admit that this error needs to be corrected. On analyzing the problem, you discover that no one else in the household eats sweets and that you could learn to be satisfied by nibbling on, let us say for example, strawberries. You decide not to buy any more candy or chocolates when you go shopping, and that you will always have some strawberries handy, all washed and ready to eat. During the daily self-hypnosis period, you visualize yourself nibbling on strawberries while watching a commercial about a new kind of candy. You generate a feeling of pride during this mental picture as you ponder how each strawberry, instead of candy, brings you closer to your goal of a slim and trim appearance. After repeatedly programming this material into your subconscious mind, ultimately you will find that you can be quite comfortable behaving in this manner during the actual bell situation.

The basic purpose of the regimen is to utilize each failure to improve yourself, rather than allowing it to serve as an excuse for saying, "What's the use—I just can't do it."

HOW TO PREVENT A RELAPSE

Probably the biggest problem of all is adhering to a maintenance diet once you have reached your ideal weight. Success may go to your head and you may decide no further restrictions are necessary to remain indefinitely at the weight you worked so hard to attain. This sort of smugness can lead to only one thing—the eventual regaining of the weight you lost. Continue to utilize what you have learned about self-hypnosis to aid you in carrying out the job of being a "weight-watcher" the rest of your life.

THIS IS A "DO IT YOURSELF" SCHEME

The responsibility is on your shoulders. If you are looking to self-hypnosis as a magic wand which will instantly help you cure your obesity, you will be disappointed. The same is true of hetero-hypnosis. As I have told you earlier, as long as you expect *someone else* to do something *to you* to lose weight, you will fail. I have presented to you a definite, specific and detailed method of self-improvement. You must practice to win this skill, but once you acquire it, you will be very richly rewarded. No portion of this regimen must be left out. You will notice that at no time have I asked you to *use your will power to stop eating.*

The procedures that you are being asked to follow are simple and efficient, but they do require continued daily practice before you can reap the maximum benefits. The results will ultimately become permanent if you do not prematurely discard the program. You will find that it is much more pleasant to work with the imagination than with will power. Eventually, the self-hypnotic conditioning sessions will only take a brief amount of your time. The keeping of the food diary takes only a few seconds for each entry, and the review of your progress once weekly takes, at the most, only one-half hour. When you have ceased to make mistakes for several months, you may discontinue the diary portion of this regimen.

You will be quite pleased when you discover, as many of my patients have found, that you can go about your daily activities without constantly having to think about your dietary habits. You will be grateful for having learned a method which does not require a constant conscious effort.

A SUMMARY OF THE TECHNIQUE

Since you should consult this chapter frequently, I have summarized the basic steps of this method for your quick reference.

(1) Learn to go into self-hypnosis and preferably practice two or more times daily. The best time is just before you go to sleep. The second session may be held at any other convenient time when you can relax undisturbed.

(2) Visualize your new self-image, wearing an attractive garment you have bought.

(3) While visualizing this self-image generate a feeling of confidence (the subconscious feel) in your ability to achieve your goal.

(4) After having achieved a clear *still* picture of the new self-image, visualize yourself actually *behaving* like a successful slim person in various pleasant situations which you have previously avoided because of your overweight.

(5) Next, visualize yourself acting properly and successfully when confronted by food. See yourself eating slowly and savoring every bite, enjoying the foods on your diet, and leaving food on your plate when you feel full.

(6) Utilize posthypnotic suggestions and condition yourself to activate the subconscious feel whenever you are tempted to go off your diet.

(7) Discover your bells, decide on a remedy for each situation, and use mental pictures during self-hypnosis to facilitate the carrying out of your correct response.

(8) Measure your week-to-week success by keeping a food diary. Do not become discouraged by temporary weight plateaus if your diary indicates that you are doing well.

(9) Discover your mistakes by a weekly review of your food diary.

(10) Learn from your failures by handling them as new bell situations and use them to your advantage for continued improvement.

(11) Do not prematurely discard the techniques after initial success.

(12) Utilize self-hypnosis as needed to remain a weight watcher the rest of your life.

(13) Use this program as an addition not a substitute, to all the other aids that your own personal physician and modern medical science have to offer you to help you with your overweight problem.

Chapter 10

Fit Your Diet to Your Needs

See Your Doctor

AN INDIVIDUAL DIET IS A MUST

It would be presumptuous and impossible to try to teach a complete course in nutrition within a few pages. There have been many volumes written on this subject and some researchers devote their lives to the study of this science. Furthermore, I have repeatedly stated a diet must be individualized by your physician. Bearing this in mind, I shall only attempt to give you a few basic principles and briefly outline my personal approach to the problems of obese patients I have seen in my own practice. Since there are always exceptions, what I say may contradict the advice of your own physician, and if it does, follow his instructions. He knows your nutritional needs better than I and, additionally, the main purpose of this book is not to tell you what to eat and what not to eat, but to describe how you can adhere to the diet which has been selected to fit your specific needs by your family physician.

The usual printed diets advocated by nutritional experts may be helpful for a majority of persons but they are usually useless when an individual attempts to put them into practice. Whenever I design a diet for a particular patient, it invariably differs from diets prescribed for other individuals with different problems. For instance, a housewife who is at home all day, active as she may be, would not be given the same diet as her husband who may earn his living by hard labor. Similarly, the diet of someone who prepares his own meals would differ from that of an individual who must eat out most of the time. Habits, the types of food you like and dislike, your general state of health, and the rapidity of weight loss desired must also all be evaluated. For permanent results, individualization of dietary regimens is an essential prerequisite.

INITIAL DIETS MUST BE RIGOROUS

In general, the initial diet should be as restrictive as the patient will accept. It is usually possible to predict how much a person will lose each month on a certain food schedule. A rapid weight loss during the first week of dieting is meaningless as it nearly always represents a loss of water. Therefore, this loss cannot be used to gauge the effectiveness of a certain regimen. However, the loss from month to month is a good indication that the diet has been properly calculated. Occasionally it becomes necessary to change dietary regimens from time to time, since a patient has changing caloric requirements as he continues to lose weight. Furthermore, he may get weary of certain foods and welcome a change in the variety of foods allowed. Unless he is an expert nutritionist, he should let his doctor make the proper modifications.

In preparing a diet for a new patient, I always ask what

he ordinarily eats when he is not dieting. I then make some alterations and discuss each change I suggest in his dietary program. Thus, we arrive at a mutually agreeable and effective schedule.

Some patients prefer to keep a detailed caloric budget from which they can choose foods at will as long as they do not go over the limit allowed. Other patients do not wish to be bothered with bookkeeping and prefer to be told that they can eat practically all they wish of certain types of foods. Still others like a middle road, using common sense to make their choices.

HOW OFTEN SHOULD YOU EAT?

The number of meals to be eaten each day is still a highly controversial subject. Most nutritionists recommend that obese individuals divide the total food they are allowed into three meals, beginning with a large breakfast. The reason usually given is that the total number of calories allowed, if distributed through the day, will account for more weight loss than if they are all lumped together in one meal. Food, especially protein, produces extra heat (the so-called "specific dynamic action") which speeds up the metabolism. This lasts only six hours after eating. Hence, a person eating three meals daily would get the "benefit" of this increased metabolism for 18 hours instead of six.

Although this sounds very scientific, in the actual practice of reducing it is only of theoretical advantage. For example, it is much easier to cheat three times daily than it is once. Since most meals represent bells for patients, avoiding these conditioned stimuli as much as possible is very helpful at the start. Later, after self-hypnosis has negated the conditioned response of overeating, it does not make any difference how often the individual is exposed to food.

119

A HELPFUL FOOD DISTRIBUTION

It has been my experience that most patients do better initially on two meals per day—one large and one small. The smaller meal is eaten early in the day, and the larger meal near the end. Most of my reducing patients have conditioned themselves to skip the noon meal. It is much easier to say to themselves, "I can wait until this evening," rather than, "I can't have any more food today because I have already consumed my quota." However, there are some exceptions. I have a number of patients who are more satisfied with five small meals a day and I have others, particularly working people, who find that they do very well on one meal per day. I am referring mainly to the initial diet which has to be drastic in order to effect an immediate weight loss and keep motivation at a high pitch. The maintenance diet is a separate type of program and may have an entirely different schedule.

An interesting result of these rearranged eating schedules, however, is that I have had a large number of patients who enjoyed their one- or two-meal-per-day schedule so much that they have made it a permanent eating habit. Many have stayed on such a regimen for several years now and found this to be an easy and pleasant way to maintain their ideal weight.

FOOD ADDICTION AND ALLERGY

One of the most fascinating aspects of nutrition and obesity is the fact that some people seem to be addicted to certain types of foods. Unfortunately, the addictive food is usually one that is relished and eaten every day. It is possible, through clinical studies, to ascertain these foods and eliminating them should help insure the success of your dietary program. If the patient is allowed to have even small amounts of them, however, the addiction is kept active. Such a food produces a "hangover" several hours after it is ingested.

Hangover symptoms (which are really a delayed allergic reaction) often come in the form of fatigue, headache, light-headedness, nervousness, depression, and a tremendous craving for more of the same food. The individual, unaware of this mechanism, "cures" the hangover by eating more of the same food. Thus, a vicious cycle is started, very similar to that of the alcoholic. If even small amounts are allowed it becomes almost impossible for the person to adhere to the diet.

If such a person can be coerced into abstaining completely and go through the withdrawal period, the addiction can be broken. Unfortunately, eating even small amounts of the foods will immediately reactivate the addiction—just as in the narcotic addict or alcoholic. If a sufficient period of time has elapsed, the first re-exposure to such a food will cause an almost immediate allergic reaction. Later, it reverts back to the delayed hangover reaction. This phenomenon can be used to advantage in proving to a patient that he is "hooked."

TWO CASE HISTORIES

The theory that some people can be allergic and become addicted to certain foods has progressed far beyond the investigative stage. Dr. Theron G. Randolph has done extensive research in this field and has offered incontrovertible evidence that the phenomenon can occur. The Keeley Institute, a sanitarium for alcoholics, has gone far enough to prove that certain foods, notably corn, can drive the alcoholic back to drink in an attempt to cure a hangover resulting from corn. The Institute became interested in this research when its records disclosed a prosperous corn farmer returned each year for the "cure" immediately after harvest time.

My own example is the wife of a prominent insurance man who was addicted to bread. I finally convinced her she should eliminate bread and wheat products from her diet, and after a difficult withdrawal period she became free of her chronic fatigue, headaches and depression.

In order to test the accuracy of my diagnosis, I asked her to eat five slices of bread on an empty stomach. The next day she reported all her distressing symptoms had returned within two hours after she had performed the experiment.

Most patients find it difficult to believe they can become addicted to food, and I sometimes have to prove the point in such dramatic fashion. If clinical examination shows you have an addictive food allergy, self-hypnosis can be of great benefit in eliminating the harmful food or foods from your diet.

PROTEIN IS BASIC IN DIETING

The foundation of most reducing diets are the protein foods. These foods should make up the largest proportion of your caloric intake. Meats, fi and fowl come under this heading. Certain dairy products can also be included here, depending on your individual taste.

Large amounts of green, leafy and yellow vegetables, properly cooked or in the form of salads, should be added to this foundation.

These foods may be complemented by a certain amount of fat, preferably unsaturated, to make the diet tasty. You will recall, earlier in this book, that a diet to be acceptable must please the taste.

Carbohydrates should be kept to a minimum in the initial diet, but they may be gradually added as augmenting foods as you approach the time a maintenance program can be instituted. They should, as much as possible, be taken in their unrefined form as found in fresh fruits and some of the vegetables. Thus, they add to the nutritional value of the diet.

Occasionally your physician may wish to add certain vitamin and mineral supplements, although it has always been my contention that you are better off getting your vitamins at the market rather than the drug store.

OTHER HELPFUL MEASURES

Your physician may want to give you drugs to curb your appetite and make your task easier at the start. He may also advise you to employ certain "tricks" to enable you to follow his prescribed regimen. I have no objection to any of these methods as long as you do not use them excessively. You must realize that they serve only as temporary crutches. As you learn more about self-hypnosis and begin to derive the beneficial effects which are bound to ensue, you will require less and less help from drugs or gimmicks. You will know when such medication ceases to be necessary for you. My patients usually exclaim, "Doctor, I don't think I need any more of these pills that take away my appetite." They invariably say this after the conditioning and visual imagery process has become so effective that it serves them better than the pills. Eventually, you will not have to rely on any chemical aids.

You may remark that this has been a very brief chapter on diet, but please remember I have consistently stated your diet must be prescribed by your physician. This chapter is meant only to acquaint you with some of the fundamentals of constructing the framework of a reducing diet. There are many books with specific dietary instructions, and I have listed some of them in the bibliography. However, it would be wise not to follow them until you have consulted with your physician.

In this connection, I also urge the reader to obtain a copy of the "POINT ·SYSTEM FOOD PROGRAM" booklet described in Chapter 12.

Chapter 11

Questions and Answers

Let a Record Help You Reduce

In lecturing on obesity to numerous groups, I have found that there are always a number of questions asked when I have finished. I have picked out the most common ones and list them here along with the answers. The manuscript of this book was also given to a number of people and their questions are also included.

Q: I have a number of friends who tell me the only way to lose weight is through will power. When I told them that I was using self-hypnosis they said it was just a new fad and wouldn't work.

A: Medical hypnosis has been officially accepted and endorsed by the American Medical Association, The British Medical Association and the American Dental Association. It is being used daily by numerous practitioners, not only in this country, but throughout the world. Actually, hypnosis is as old as medicine itself, and has been used under various labels for centuries. If the use of will power alone could help you to lose weight, your question would be unnecessary.

The reason this subject has not been given the serious consideration it deserves is because of the misconceptions fostered by fiction writers, playwrights and even those who should know better, and that, unfortunately, includes some physicians. The nonsensical stunts of stage hypnotists have also hampered general public acceptance of this modality. The doctors who speak out against hypnosis are usually the ones who remain misinformed and consequently are unable to appreciate its substantial therapeutic value.

Q: I have read books on hypnosis and I believe that I cannot be hypnotized or hypnotize myself.

A: I recommend that you learn how medical hypnosis really works. This will explain how everyone, including yourself, is hypnotized daily without realizing it. The reason some people cannot be formally hypnotized is because of fear. When unfounded anxiety is eliminated, you will have no difficulty in entering the state of hypnosis.

Q: I am afraid that if I am hypnotized too often my will may become weakened.

A: Your question indicates you do not comprehend the basic principles of hypnosis. Will power has nothing to do with hypnosis. It is through the use of the *imagination* that a person can take advantage of the many beneficial effects of the hypnotic state. In fact, anyone who learns self-hypnosis will actually enhance his will power because it enables him to perform acts of will he formerly found impossible. I personally use self-hypnosis daily and would not be able to accomplish half the things I do without its aid.

Q: I have lost weight easily using self-hypnosis, but now I am beginning to gain it back. What did I do wrong?

A: If you will read the section in Chapter Nine that deals with relapses you will realize that you have failed to avoid the main pitfall of this system. You did not follow the suggested methods long enough. If you had persevered, you would not be regaining weight.

Q: I have experienced some difficulty in entering a satisfactory state of self-hypnosis. Because of this, I do not believe that I am getting the benefits that I should.

A: First consult your doctor. He may either use hypnosis himself or refer you to a physician experienced in the use of this modality in obesity. As I have said previously, it is more difficult to learn a skill from a book than it is from personal instruction. If you are not able to find a good hypnotist, you can contact your local medical society for the names of competent men in your area.

To assist you in learning self-hypnosis for reducing purposes, I have made a special record. This can serve as an added aid to personal instruction by a hypnotist or your own efforts. For further details read the answer to the last question in this chapter.

Q: I have asked my doctor if he objects to my use of self-hypnosis to reduce weight. He has told me that this method is controversial.

A: I advise you to ask your doctor to read this book. If, after reading it, he still feels that you should not use self-hypnosis, I would appreciate it if you would tell him to write to me (care of the publisher of this book) and raise his objections. I can refer him to numerous scientific publications in medical journals which will assure him of the value of this modality. Nevertheless, in the meantime, you should abide by his advice since you are under his medical care. Remember, however, that self-hypnosis will not replace his present program. It simply will be an added help.

Q: Why can't I use the power of positive thinking instead of self-hypnosis? I can't see any difference between the two.

A: These two terms are often confused. In self-hypnosis, you are actually using your subconscious mind to improve yourself. Positive thinking utilizes only your conscious mind. With the latter, it is much more difficult to achieve results and takes more time. Nevertheless, if you wish, you can combine the two methods.

Q: I do not believe that I have sufficient time to utilize self-hypnosis in the way that you have described. What can I do?

A: My specific and detailed plan of handling your obesity problem may take longer initially but it will save you much more time in the long run and avoid the recurrent up-and-down fluctuations in weight typical of the usual reducing attempts. When you become adept, you will find that you can hypnotize yourself in seconds and accomplish far more than you can now. For example, in my own case, with an extremely busy medical practice, I would never have been able to write this book without the aid of self-hypnosis. Lack of time would have been too difficult a problem. You will be amazed at your increased efficiency when you use self-hypnosis.

Q. I was told by a friend that hypnosis is against my religion. Is this true if I only use it to help me reduce?

A: All the major religions agree that hypnosis is a natural phenomenon which we can use to benefit ourselves. Many clergymen have used the principles of hypnosis for years. There are many references in the Bible to the manifestations of this state.

Questions and Answers

Q: Is hypnosis all I need to make me lose weight? Is there any other knowledge I must have first before applying it properly?

A: Yes, you must be aware of the energy value of foods. The next chapter describes this in more detail.

Q: I have heard there is a record that teaches you self-hypnosis and then helps you to program constructive posthypnotic suggestions into the subconscious mind for dieting. Is there such a record and can it be effective?

A: Yes, I have made such a record and mentioned it earlier in this chapter. It can be extremely effective in helping you learn to induce self-hypnosis for dieting. The record was made at the request of many persons who read the manuscript of this book and wished to condition themselves to enter into the hypnotic state and who also wished to have my special tips on dieting made available for listening.

After you have become relaxed by following the suggestions on the first part of the record, you will find that you are memorizing all the other suggestions with little or no effort on your part. Within a short time your ability to control your diet will be automatic proof that your subconscious is helping you diet.

What this record really does is to help you to change your faulty eating habits. Your subconscious mind has been conditioned to react improperly to the stimuli of fattening foods. These memory patterns are altered by repeated suggestions to correct responses so that your appetite is not activated when previously detrimental stimuli are encountered. Additionally, you will find you are acting on suggestions calculated to generate the proper positive mental attitude toward reducing. Your self-image will become one of dynamic confidence and you will develop the self-esteem necessary to diet with a minimum of difficulty.

The record is called *Mind Over Platter* and sells for $7.00 postpaid. It is also available on cassette and sells for $11.00 postpaid. Either can be obtained directly from Wilshire Book Company, 12015 Sherman Road, North Hollywood, California 91605.

Chapter 12

Eat All You Want, Enjoy It And Lose
The "Point System"

The major portion of this book has been devoted to a description of the theory and method of learning and becoming more proficient at the skills necessary for lifelong adherence to an eating program specifically tailored to your needs. As you know, I have repeatedly urged you to obtain specific information on *what* you should eat from your personal physician.

Nevertheless, there is a basic rule which applies to all individuals, one which all the new knowledge of medicine has never disproved and that rule simply states, "If an individual reduces his energy intake below his energy output, he will lose fat." Thus, it is an indispensable fact that every person on a weight control program must be aware of—and constantly heed—the fuel value of foods.

Since the only thing that counts in losing weight is the amount of *fuel* you take into your body, you must constantly ask yourself, "How much fuel am I taking in?" Trying to gauge this by the *amount* of food you eat is not necessarily indicative of the amount of fuel you are getting. You could actually eat a very small amount of food—not enough to appease your hunger—but still gain weight because of its high fuel value.

On the other hand, many of my patients eat plentifully, but because their total fuel intake—totalled at the end of each week—is less than they expend, they lose weight in the process.

It became apparent to me many years ago that most persons with a weight problem—and that unfortunately includes numerous members of the medical profession—are completely unaware of the true energy value of foods. Since this fuel value is the *only* thing that counts in the loss of fat and in preventing it from being regained, I realized that a simple method of quickly estimating how much fuel was being consumed was badly needed.

Keeping track of calories (our standard way of measuring the energy value of foods) is too complicated and time-consuming. In addition, many available books, even the recent ones, are inaccurate, confusing and vary markedly in their tables of food values.

Because of the variances, I found it necessary to develop a system I call the *Point System of Relative Food Values*. It has been used by innumerable patients, repeatedly revised and brought up to date from the most authoritative sources, and simplified until it has become the most accurate and practical method in use. It has stood the test of time and proved its value in all types of individuals. Persons who have used it have invariably commented on its extreme simplicity, and the considerable amount of necessary knowledge they have gained in using the system. One of the major advantages of this method (one that is absolutely necessary for lifelong weight control) is that there are no prohibitions. There is literally nothing you cannot eat. You have complete freedom in your choice of foods. On restricted diets, you are always looking forward to the day when the ban will be lifted. When this day arrives, regaining the weight is almost inevitable because the formerly forbidden foods prove an irresistible temptation.

With the *Point System* there are no such frustrating restrictions. You can have anything you want, as long as you can work it into your alloted weekly (not daily) allowance of total points (fuel value). It is somewhat like an expense account. You can spend it any way that you like.

Once they master the *Point System,* my patients have always discovered how they can manage to maintain their correct weight and still include the foods they enjoy and would not like to give up. When learning to change their daily eating habits, this knowledge of the energy value of foods has also been of immeasurable aid.

Until recently, the use of the *System* has been restricted to my own patients. But because of its remarkable reception and persistent requests from those attending my many obesity lectures, I have finally published the complete *Point System* in booklet form, small enough to be carried in a shirt pocket or purse. This booklet is being used by many other physicians and their patients with equal success, and the response has been exceptional.

In bringing this book to a close, I feel obligated to make this invaluable aid available to the reader of *Mind Over Platter.*

Briefly, the *Point System* eliminates the chore of tiresome and variable methods of calculating calories, yet gives you the same information. It is so simple you can quickly and accurately count food values in your head, since most foods are valued from only 1 to 20 points. There are no complicated figures to remember or add up. It is learned very quickly and tells you exactly where you stand at any time of the day as to how much fuel you have consumed thus far.

For example, if you use the food diary suggested in these pages, you will find it a simple matter to enter the point value after each food you have eaten. Thus, you will not only know how much *food* you have consumed at the end of the week, but also how much energy you have put into your body. As I have stated previously, it is only the latter which is of importance in control of body fat, and this *System* will allow you to plan intelligently to eat foods you enjoy without being a mathematical genius or use involved calculations. After all, eating is one of life's chief pleasures, and you might as well enjoy it while you attain and maintain your new slim, trim goal.

The booklet is entitled: *Dr. Lindner's Point System Food Program* and may be obtained by sending $3.00 to:

Wilshire Book Company
12015 Sherman Road
No. Hollywood, California 91605

Appendix

BIBLIOGRAPHY

The following books are suggested for supplementary reading and may be obtained from the Wilshire Book Company or your local bookstore.

Further reading on self-hypnosis:

1. A PRACTICAL GUIDE TO SELF-HYPNOSIS by Melvin Powers.
2. SELF-HYPNOSIS Its Theory, Technique & Application by Melvin Powers.
3. HELPING YOURSELF WITH SELF-HYPNOSIS by Frank S. Caprio, M. D.
4. WHAT IS HYPNOSIS by Andrew Salter.
5. AUTO-CONDITIONING: THE NEW WAY TO A SUCCESSFUL LIFE by Hornell Hart, Ph. D.

For those readers more technically minded, especially professional people working in this field, the following books are highly recommended:

1. CLINICAL AND EXPERIMENTAL HYPNOSIS by William S. Kroger, M. D.
2. PSYCHOTHERAPY BY RECIPROCAL INHIBITION by Joseph Wolpe, M.D.
3. THE WORD — AS A PHYSIOLOGICAL AND THERAPEUTIC FACTOR by K. Platonov, M. D.
4. MEDICAL HYPNOSIS HANDBOOK By Drs. Van Pelt, Ambrose & Newbold.
5. MODERN HYPNOSIS by Lesley Kuhn & Frank Russo, Ph. D.
6. HYPNOSIS AND ITS THERAPEUTIC APPLICATIONS edited by Roy M. Dorcus, Ph. D.

Further reading about foods and nutrition:

1. DR. LINDNER'S POINT SYSTEM FOOD PROGRAM
   by Peter G. Lindner, M.D. & Daisy C. Lindner, R.N.
2. STOP DIETING AND START LOSING by Ruth West.
3. REDUCE AND STAY REDUCED by Norman Jolliffe, M.D.

Listed below are some related books on subjects which are extremely interesting to persons wishing to learn more about how we are conditioned by suggestion:

1. PSYCHO-CYBERNETICS by Maxwell Maltz, M. D.
2. THE HIDDEN PERSUADERS by Vance Packard.
3. THE BATTLE FOR THE MIND by William Sargant.
4. SELF-MASTERY THROUGH CONSCIOUS AUTO-SUGGESTION by Emile Coué.
5. SUGGESTION AND AUTO-SUGGESTION by Charles Baudouin.
6. HYPNOTISM — An Objective Study in Suggestibility
   by André M. Weitzenhoffer, Ph. D.
7. MEDICAL HYPNOSIS by Lewis R. Wolberg, M. D.
8. TIME DISTORTION IN HYPNOSIS
   by Milton H. Erickson, M. D. & Linn F. Cooper, M. D.
9. A PRACTICAL GUIDE TO BETTER CONCENTRATION
   by Melvin Powers & Robert S. Starrett.

SUGGESTED FORM FOR DIET DIARY

DATE							
DAY OF WEEK	MONDAY	TUESDAY	WEDNESDAY	THURSDAY	FRIDAY	SATURDAY	SUNDAY
BREAKFAST							
LUNCH							
DINNER							

SUGGESTED FORM FOR DIET DIARY

DATE							
DAY OF WEEK	MONDAY	TUESDAY	WEDNESDAY	THURSDAY	FRIDAY	SATURDAY	SUNDAY
BREAKFAST							
LUNCH							
DINNER							

MELVIN POWERS SELF-IMPROVEMENT LIBRARY

ASTROLOGY

_____ASTROLOGY: HOW TO CHART YOUR HOROSCOPE *Max Heindel* 3.00
_____ASTROLOGY: YOUR PERSONAL SUN-SIGN GUIDE *Beatrice Ryder* 3.00
_____ASTROLOGY FOR EVERYDAY LIVING *Janet Harris* 2.00
_____ASTROLOGY MADE EASY *Astarte* 3.00
_____ASTROLOGY MADE PRACTICAL *Alexandra Kayhle* 3.00
_____ASTROLOGY, ROMANCE, YOU AND THE STARS *Anthony Norvell* 4.00
_____MY WORLD OF ASTROLOGY *Sydney Omarr* 5.00
_____THOUGHT DIAL *Sydney Omarr* 3.00
_____WHAT THE STARS REVEAL ABOUT THE MEN IN YOUR LIFE *Thelma White* 3.00

BRIDGE

_____BRIDGE BIDDING MADE EASY *Edwin B. Kantar* 5.00
_____BRIDGE CONVENTIONS *Edwin B. Kantar* 5.00
_____BRIDGE HUMOR *Edwin B. Kantar* 3.00
_____COMPETITIVE BIDDING IN MODERN BRIDGE *Edgar Kaplan* 4.00
_____DEFENSIVE BRIDGE PLAY COMPLETE *Edwin B. Kantar* 10.00
_____HOW TO IMPROVE YOUR BRIDGE *Alfred Sheinwold* 3.00
_____IMPROVING YOUR BIDDING SKILLS *Edwin B. Kantar* 4.00
_____INTRODUCTION TO DEFENDER'S PLAY *Edwin B. Kantar* 3.00
_____SHORT CUT TO WINNING BRIDGE *Alfred Sheinwold* 3.00
_____TEST YOUR BRIDGE PLAY *Edwin B. Kantar* 3.00
_____WINNING DECLARER PLAY *Dorothy Hayden Truscott* 4.00

BUSINESS, STUDY & REFERENCE

_____CONVERSATION MADE EASY *Elliot Russell* 2.00
_____EXAM SECRET *Dennis B. Jackson* 3.00
_____FIX-IT BOOK *Arthur Symons* 2.00
_____HOW TO DEVELOP A BETTER SPEAKING VOICE *M. Hellier* 3.00
_____HOW TO MAKE A FORTUNE IN REAL ESTATE *Albert Winnikoff* 4.00
_____INCREASE YOUR LEARNING POWER *Geoffrey A. Dudley* 2.00
_____MAGIC OF NUMBERS *Robert Tocquet* 2.00
_____PRACTICAL GUIDE TO BETTER CONCENTRATION *Melvin Powers* 3.00
_____PRACTICAL GUIDE TO PUBLIC SPEAKING *Maurice Forley* 3.00
_____7 DAYS TO FASTER READING *William S. Schaill* 3.00
_____SONGWRITERS RHYMING DICTIONARY *Jane Shaw Whitfield* 5.00
_____SPELLING MADE EASY *Lester D. Basch & Dr. Milton Finkelstein* 2.00
_____STUDENT'S GUIDE TO BETTER GRADES *J. A. Rickard* 3.00
_____TEST YOURSELF—Find Your Hidden Talent *Jack Shafer* 3.00
_____YOUR WILL & WHAT TO DO ABOUT IT *Attorney Samuel G. Kling* 3.00

CALLIGRAPHY

_____ADVANCED CALLIGRAPHY *Katherine Jeffares* 7.00
_____CALLIGRAPHER'S REFERENCE BOOK *Anne Leptich & Jacque Evans* 6.00
_____CALLIGRAPHY—The Art of Beautiful Writing *Katherine Jeffares* 6.00
_____CALLIGRAPHY FOR FUN & PROFIT *Anne Leptich & Jacque Evans* 6.00

CHESS & CHECKERS

_____BEGINNER'S GUIDE TO WINNING CHESS *Fred Reinfeld* 3.00
_____BETTER CHESS—How to Play *Fred Reinfeld* 2.00
_____CHECKERS MADE EASY *Tom Wiswell* 2.00
_____CHESS IN TEN EASY LESSONS *Larry Evans* 3.00
_____CHESS MADE EASY *Milton L. Hanauer* 3.00
_____CHESS MASTERY—A New Approach *Fred Reinfeld* 3.00
_____CHESS PROBLEMS FOR BEGINNERS *edited by Fred Reinfeld* 2.00
_____CHESS SECRETS REVEALED *Fred Reinfeld* 2.00
_____CHESS STRATEGY—An Expert's Guide *Fred Reinfeld* 2.00
_____CHESS TACTICS FOR BEGINNERS *edited by Fred Reinfeld* 3.00
_____CHESS THEORY & PRACTICE *Morry & Mitchell* 2.00
_____HOW TO WIN AT CHECKERS *Fred Reinfeld* 3.00
_____1001 BRILLIANT WAYS TO CHECKMATE *Fred Reinfeld* 3.00
_____1001 WINNING CHESS SACRIFICES & COMBINATIONS *Fred Reinfeld* 3.00
_____SOVIET CHESS *Edited by R. G. Wade* 3.00

COOKERY & HERBS

_____CULPEPER'S HERBAL REMEDIES *Dr. Nicholas Culpeper* 3.00

FAST GOURMET COOKBOOK *Poppy Cannon*	2.50
GINSENG The Myth & The Truth *Joseph P. Hou*	3.00
HEALING POWER OF HERBS *May Bethel*	3.00
HEALING POWER OF NATURAL FOODS *May Bethel*	3.00
HERB HANDBOOK *Dawn MacLeod*	3.00
HERBS FOR COOKING AND HEALING *Dr. Donald Law*	2.00
HERBS FOR HEALTH—How to Grow & Use Them *Louise Evans Doole*	3.00
HOME GARDEN COOKBOOK—Delicious Natural Food Recipes *Ken Kraft*	3.00
MEDICAL HERBALIST *edited by Dr. J. R. Yemm*	3.00
NATURAL FOOD COOKBOOK *Dr. Harry C. Bond*	3.00
NATURE'S MEDICINES *Richard Lucas*	3.00
VEGETABLE GARDENING FOR BEGINNERS *Hugh Wiberg*	2.00
VEGETABLES FOR TODAY'S GARDENS *R. Milton Carleton*	2.00
VEGETARIAN COOKERY *Janet Walker*	3.00
VEGETARIAN COOKING MADE EASY & DELECTABLE *Veronica Vezza*	3.00
VEGETARIAN DELIGHTS—A Happy Cookbook for Health *K. R. Mehta*	2.00
VEGETARIAN GOURMET COOKBOOK *Joyce McKinnel*	3.00

GAMBLING & POKER

ADVANCED POKER STRATEGY & WINNING PLAY *A. D. Livingston*	3.00
HOW NOT TO LOSE AT POKER *Jeffrey Lloyd Castle*	3.00
HOW TO WIN AT DICE GAMES *Skip Frey*	3.00
HOW TO WIN AT POKER *Terence Reese & Anthony T. Watkins*	3.00
SECRETS OF WINNING POKER *George S. Coffin*	3.00
WINNING AT CRAPS *Dr. Lloyd T. Commins*	3.00
WINNING AT GIN *Chester Wander & Cy Rice*	3.00
WINNING AT POKER—An Expert's Guide *John Archer*	3.00
WINNING AT 21—An Expert's Guide *John Archer*	3.00
WINNING POKER SYSTEMS *Norman Zadeh*	3.00

HEALTH

BEE POLLEN *Lynda Lyngheim & Jack Scagnetti*	3.00
DR. LINDNER'S SPECIAL WEIGHT CONTROL METHOD *P. G. Lindner, M.D.*	1.50
HELP YOURSELF TO BETTER SIGHT *Margaret Darst Corbett*	3.00
HOW TO IMPROVE YOUR VISION *Dr. Robert A. Kraskin*	3.00
HOW YOU CAN STOP SMOKING PERMANENTLY *Ernest Caldwell*	3.00
MIND OVER PLATTER *Peter G. Lindner, M.D.*	3.00
NATURE'S WAY TO NUTRITION & VIBRANT HEALTH *Robert J. Scrutton*	3.00
NEW CARBOHYDRATE DIET COUNTER *Patti Lopez-Pereira*	1.50
PSYCHEDELIC ECSTASY *William Marshall & Gilbert W. Taylor*	2.00
QUICK & EASY EXERCISES FOR FACIAL BEAUTY *Judy Smith-deal*	2.00
QUICK & EASY EXERCISES FOR FIGURE BEAUTY *Judy Smith-deal*	2.00
REFLEXOLOGY *Dr. Maybelle Segal*	3.00
REFLEXOLOGY FOR GOOD HEALTH *Anna Kaye & Don C. Matchan*	3.00
YOU CAN LEARN TO RELAX *Dr. Samuel Gutwirth*	3.00
YOUR ALLERGY—What To Do About It *Allan Knight, M.D.*	3.00

HOBBIES

BEACHCOMBING FOR BEGINNERS *Norman Hickin*	2.00
BLACKSTONE'S MODERN CARD TRICKS *Harry Blackstone*	3.00
BLACKSTONE'S SECRETS OF MAGIC *Harry Blackstone*	2.00
COIN COLLECTING FOR BEGINNERS *Burton Hobson & Fred Reinfeld*	3.00
ENTERTAINING WITH ESP *Tony 'Doc' Shiels*	2.00
400 FASCINATING MAGIC TRICKS YOU CAN DO *Howard Thurston*	3.00
HOW I TURN JUNK INTO FUN AND PROFIT *Sari*	3.00
HOW TO PLAY THE HARMONICA FOR FUN & PROFIT *Hal Leighton*	3.00
HOW TO WRITE A HIT SONG & SELL IT *Tommy Boyce*	7.00
JUGGLING MADE EASY *Rudolf Dittrich*	2.00
MAGIC MADE EASY *Byron Wels*	2.00
STAMP COLLECTING FOR BEGINNERS *Burton Hobson*	2.00

HORSE PLAYERS' WINNING GUIDES

BETTING HORSES TO WIN *Les Conklin*	3.00
ELIMINATE THE LOSERS *Bob McKnight*	3.00
HOW TO PICK WINNING HORSES *Bob McKnight*	3.00
HOW TO WIN AT THE RACES *Sam (The Genius) Lewin*	3.00

MELVIN POWERS' MAIL ORDER LIBRARY

_____HOW TO GET RICH IN MAIL ORDER *Melvin Powers*	10.00
_____HOW TO WRITE A GOOD ADVERTISEMENT *Victor O. Schwab*	15.00
_____WORLD WIDE MAIL ORDER SHOPPER'S GUIDE *Eugene V. Moller*	5.00

METAPHYSICS & OCCULT

_____BOOK OF TALISMANS, AMULETS & ZODIACAL GEMS *William Pavitt*	4.00
_____CONCENTRATION—A Guide to Mental Mastery *Mouni Sadhu*	3.00
_____CRITIQUES OF GOD *Edited by Peter Angeles*	7.00
_____DREAMS & OMENS REVEALED *Fred Gettings*	3.00
_____EXTRA-TERRESTRIAL INTELLIGENCE—The First Encounter	6.00
_____FORTUNE TELLING WITH CARDS *P. Foli*	3.00
_____HANDWRITING ANALYSIS MADE EASY *John Marley*	3.00
_____HANDWRITING TELLS *Nadya Olyanova*	5.00
_____HOW TO UNDERSTAND YOUR DREAMS *Geoffrey A. Dudley*	3.00
_____ILLUSTRATED YOGA *William Zorn*	3.00
_____IN DAYS OF GREAT PEACE *Mouni Sadhu*	3.00
_____KING SOLOMON'S TEMPLE IN THE MASONIC TRADITION *Alex Horne*	5.00
_____LSD—THE AGE OF MIND *Bernard Roseman*	2.00
_____MAGICIAN—His training and work *W. E. Butler*	3.00
_____MEDITATION *Mouni Sadhu*	4.00
_____MODERN NUMEROLOGY *Morris C. Goodman*	3.00
_____NUMEROLOGY—ITS FACTS AND SECRETS *Ariel Yvon Taylor*	3.00
_____NUMEROLOGY MADE EASY *W. Mykian*	3.00
_____PALMISTRY MADE EASY *Fred Gettings*	3.00
_____PALMISTRY MADE PRACTICAL *Elizabeth Daniels Squire*	3.00
_____PALMISTRY SECRETS REVEALED *Henry Frith*	3.00
_____PRACTICAL YOGA *Ernest Wood*	3.00
_____PROPHECY IN OUR TIME *Martin Ebon*	2.50
_____PSYCHOLOGY OF HANDWRITING *Nadya Olyanova*	3.00
_____SUPERSTITION—Are you superstitious? *Eric Maple*	2.00
_____TAROT *Mouni Sadhu*	5.00
_____TAROT OF THE BOHEMIANS *Papus*	5.00
_____TEST YOUR ESP *Martin Ebon*	2.00
_____WAYS TO SELF-REALIZATION *Mouni Sadhu*	3.00
_____WHAT YOUR HANDWRITING REVEALS *Albert E. Hughes*	2.00
_____WITCHCRAFT, MAGIC & OCCULTISM—A Fascinating History *W. B. Crow*	5.00
_____WITCHCRAFT—THE SIXTH SENSE *Justine Glass*	3.00
_____WORLD OF PSYCHIC RESEARCH *Hereward Carrington*	2.00

SELF-HELP & INSPIRATIONAL

_____CYBERNETICS WITHIN US *Y. Saparina*	3.00
_____DAILY POWER FOR JOYFUL LIVING *Dr. Donald Curtis*	3.00
_____DYNAMIC THINKING *Melvin Powers*	2.00
_____EXUBERANCE—Your Guide to Happiness & Fulfillment *Dr. Paul Kurtz*	3.00
_____GREATEST POWER IN THE UNIVERSE *U. S. Andersen*	4.00
_____GROW RICH WHILE YOU SLEEP *Ben Sweetland*	3.00
_____GROWTH THROUGH REASON *Albert Ellis, Ph.D.*	4.00
_____GUIDE TO DEVELOPING YOUR POTENTIAL *Herbert A. Otto, Ph.D.*	3.00
_____GUIDE TO LIVING IN BALANCE *Frank S. Caprio, M.D.*	2.00
_____HELPING YOURSELF WITH APPLIED PSYCHOLOGY *R. Henderson*	2.00
_____HELPING YOURSELF WITH PSYCHIATRY *Frank S. Caprio, M.D.*	2.00
_____HOW TO ATTRACT GOOD LUCK *A. H. Z. Carr*	3.00
_____HOW TO CONTROL YOUR DESTINY *Norvell*	3.00
_____HOW TO DEVELOP A WINNING PERSONALITY *Martin Panzer*	3.00
_____HOW TO DEVELOP AN EXCEPTIONAL MEMORY *Young & Gibson*	4.00
_____HOW TO OVERCOME YOUR FEARS *M. P. Leahy, M.D.*	3.00
_____HOW YOU CAN HAVE CONFIDENCE AND POWER *Les Giblin*	3.00
_____HUMAN PROBLEMS & HOW TO SOLVE THEM *Dr. Donald Curtis*	3.00
_____I CAN *Ben Sweetland*	4.00
_____I WILL *Ben Sweetland*	3.00
_____LEFT-HANDED PEOPLE *Michael Barsley*	4.00
_____MAGIC IN YOUR MIND *U. S. Andersen*	4.00
_____MAGIC OF THINKING BIG *Dr. David J. Schwartz*	3.00
_____MAGIC POWER OF YOUR MIND *Walter M. Germain*	4.00

_____MENTAL POWER THROUGH SLEEP SUGGESTION *Melvin Powers*   3.00
_____NEW GUIDE TO RATIONAL LIVING *Albert Ellis, Ph.D. & R. Harper, Ph.D.*   3.00
_____OUR TROUBLED SELVES *Dr. Allan Fromme*   3.00
_____PSYCHO-CYBERNETICS *Maxwell Maltz, M.D.*   2.00
_____SCIENCE OF MIND IN DAILY LIVING *Dr. Donald Curtis*   3.00
_____SECRET OF SECRETS *U. S. Andersen*   4.00
_____SECRET POWER OF THE PYRAMIDS *U. S. Andersen*   4.00
_____STUTTERING AND WHAT YOU CAN DO ABOUT IT *W. Johnson, Ph.D.*   2.50
_____SUCCESS-CYBERNETICS *U. S. Andersen*   4.00
_____10 DAYS TO A GREAT NEW LIFE *William E. Edwards*   3.00
_____THINK AND GROW RICH *Napoleon Hill*   3.00
_____THREE MAGIC WORDS *U. S. Andersen*   5.00
_____TREASURY OF COMFORT *edited by Rabbi Sidney Greenberg*   5.00
_____TREASURY OF THE ART OF LIVING *Sidney S. Greenberg*   5.00
_____YOU ARE NOT THE TARGET *Laura Huxley*   4.00
_____YOUR SUBCONSCIOUS POWER *Charles M. Simmons*   4.00
_____YOUR THOUGHTS CAN CHANGE YOUR LIFE *Dr. Donald Curtis*   3.00

SPORTS

_____ARCHERY—An Expert's Guide *Dan Stamp*   2.00
_____BICYCLING FOR FUN AND GOOD HEALTH *Kenneth E. Luther*   2.00
_____BILLIARDS—Pocket • Carom • Three Cushion *Clive Cottingham, Jr.*   3.00
_____CAMPING-OUT 101 Ideas & Activities *Bruno Knobel*   2.00
_____COMPLETE GUIDE TO FISHING *Vlad Evanoff*   2.00
_____HOW TO IMPROVE YOUR RACQUETBALL *Lubarsky, Kaufman, & Scagnetti*   3.00
_____HOW TO WIN AT POCKET BILLIARDS *Edward D. Knuchell*   4.00
_____JOY OF WALKING *Jack Scagnetti*   3.00
_____LEARNING & TEACHING SOCCER SKILLS *Eric Worthington*   3.00
_____MOTORCYCLING FOR BEGINNERS *I. G. Edmonds*   3.00
_____RACQUETBALL FOR WOMEN *Toni Hudson, Jack Scagnetti & Vince Rondone*   3.00
_____RACQUETBALL MADE EASY *Steve Lubarsky, Rod Delson & Jack Scagnetti*   3.00
_____SECRET OF BOWLING STRIKES *Dawson Taylor*   3.00
_____SECRET OF PERFECT PUTTING *Horton Smith & Dawson Taylor*   3.00
_____SOCCER—The game & how to play it *Gary Rosenthal*   3.00
_____STARTING SOCCER *Edward F. Dolan, Jr.*   3.00
_____TABLE TENNIS MADE EASY *Johnny Leach*   2.00

TENNIS LOVERS' LIBRARY

_____BEGINNER'S GUIDE TO WINNING TENNIS *Helen Hull Jacobs*   2.00
_____HOW TO BEAT BETTER TENNIS PLAYERS *Loring Fiske*   4.00
_____HOW TO IMPROVE YOUR TENNIS—Style, Strategy & Analysis *C. Wilson*   2.00
_____INSIDE TENNIS—Techniques of Winning *Jim Leighton*   3.00
_____PLAY TENNIS WITH ROSEWALL *Ken Rosewall*   2.00
_____PSYCH YOURSELF TO BETTER TENNIS *Dr. Walter A. Luszki*   2.00
_____SUCCESSFUL TENNIS *Neale Fraser*   2.00
_____TENNIS FOR BEGINNERS *Dr. H. A. Murray*   2.00
_____TENNIS MADE EASY *Joel Brecheen*   2.00
_____WEEKEND TENNIS—How to have fun & win at the same time *Bill Talbert*   3.00
_____WINNING WITH PERCENTAGE TENNIS—Smart Strategy *Jack Lowe*   2.00

WILSHIRE PET LIBRARY

_____DOG OBEDIENCE TRAINING *Gust Kessopulos*   3.00
_____DOG TRAINING MADE EASY & FUN *John W. Kellogg*   3.00
_____HOW TO BRING UP YOUR PET DOG *Kurt Unkelbach*   2.0
_____HOW TO RAISE & TRAIN YOUR PUPPY *Jeff Griffen*   2.0
_____PIGEONS: HOW TO RAISE & TRAIN THEM *William H. Allen, Jr.*   2.0

*The books listed above can be obtained from your book dealer or directly from
Melvin Powers. When ordering, please remit 50¢ per book postage & handling.
Send for our free illustrated catalog of self-improvement books.*

Melvin Powers
12015 Sherman Road, No. Hollywood, California 91605